Growing Up with My Children

Growing Up with My Children

Reflections of a Less-Than-Perfect Parent

Ellen Walker

Hazelden ®

First published April, 1988.

Copyright © 1988, Hazelden Foundation.
All rights reserved. No portion of this publication
may be reproduced in any manner without the written
permission of the publisher.

ISBN: 0-89486-515-3

Library of Congress Catalog Card Number:
87-83541

Printed in the United States of America.

Editor's Note:
Hazelden Educational Materials offers a variety of information on chemical dependency and related areas. Our publica-
tions do not necessarily represent Hazelden or its programs, nor
do they officially speak for any Twelve Step organization.

To my husband, Jim,
and our children, Tonya, Kevin, and Todd
with gratitude for their love, support, and understanding

Acknowledgments

This book is dedicated to my husband and children. They willingly forfeited our family time as I was writing this book. An even greater contribution, however, was their willingness to have portions of their lives and experiences be the basis of these reflections.

A large circle of understanding people encouraged me in many ways. Friends and relatives were understanding about my withdrawal from the world and still listened patiently when I resurfaced to read my essays to them: Thank you Mom, Aunt Lil, Bette, Ev, Terry, Donna, Keith, Sarona, and Bev.

I also want to thank the editorial staff at Hazelden Educational Materials, especially Judy Delaney who edited the book, Scott Zins who designed the book, and Linda Peterson and Terry Spohn who encouraged my writing, for their technical and emotional support.

Contents

Man is the only animal that laughs and weeps; for he is the only animal that is struck with the difference between what things are and what they might have been.

—William Hazlitt

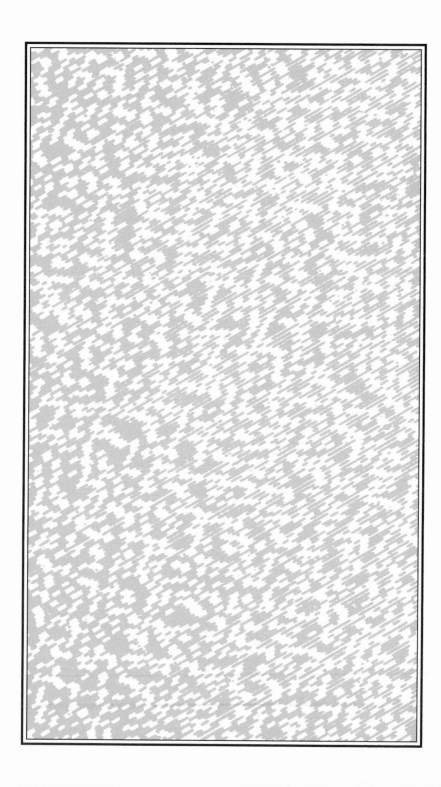

Introduction

No single event can awaken within us a stranger totally unknown to us. To live is to be slowly born.
                              —Saint-Exupery

Parenting started out as a serious business for me. I expected it to somehow transform me into what I'd always wanted to be and had always wanted others to think me to be—perfect. It's cleansing, but embarrassing, to admit that I, at the time a woman in her late twenties, had actually expected—not just a baby—but a miracle.

A good share of my parenting years was spent on regret, anger, and self-recrimination. At times, I felt I was the only parent in the world who was tired and impatient. My sense of frustration was sometimes so great that the skills I did have were decreased. I was afraid I'd taken on more than I could handle, but I never mentioned it to anyone because I was even more afraid that other parents would look at me in puzzlement and say, "I have no idea what you're talking about. I've never felt that way. I love my children."

There was no one magic moment in which I suddenly realized I wasn't unique in my fear, loneliness, and frustration. No single event. Unless it was maturity, a slow awakening and acceptance of myself. However and whenever it came, there was also a wondrous freedom accompanying it. I was freed of the rigorous need to defend and pretend and became open to growth and change.

About that time, I joined a parenting group. It was the first time I heard other parents talking about the self-doubts and fears that I thought were mine alone. The group was very informal; we usually just talked about

1

what was happening in our families. The topics ranged from minor to major events, from the appropriate age for daughters (or sons) to pierce their ears to pregnancy and chemical dependency. Whatever parental concerns we aired, the overriding tone of our evenings was one of support. "Trust yourself," we'd say, or "You're doing the best you can." Like any other support group, our purpose was not to direct another's life; our goal was to affirm each other's worth and to offer understanding. We'd share insights about problems, often by telling of similar circumstances in our families. If this sharing provided our friends with new hope or with a better understanding of themselves, that was an added benefit. But primarily we met because we found comfort in each other and in the opportunity to be totally honest. We shed our pretenses of perfection.

No person wears but one hat. I am not just a parent. I am also a wife, a daughter, a sister, a friend, a god-parent, and on and on. I'm also something else that defies a title or name; there's a me that carries forward an individual sense of being that has been with me—that has *been* me—since I can remember. I'm not a perfect parent, nor am I a perfect anything. But I am, like every other human on the face of this earth, being "slowly born." I'm becoming. Becoming less selfish. Becoming more tolerant and patient. Becoming more understanding and accepting of others—and myself.

This honesty and acceptance of imperfection have helped me deal with guilt and regret. Although I still waste time wishing I were a better parent, I realize now that wishes and regrets can change nothing. In fact, they have often rooted me in one spot and prevented the very growth and change needed for better parenting. I've made many mistakes, and not one of them can be changed. What can be changed is me, so tomorrow I can be a better person and, therefore, a better parent, daughter, and wife.

Much of the material included here was intended to be letters to my children, an attempt to explain myself to them. I wanted them to know that my muddled attempts at parenting weren't reflections or measurements of my love for them. But seventeen years of parenting—seventeen years of growth—has given me many gifts, and the most important of those is acceptance of myself as less than perfect. What I've written is no longer for my children; it's for me and other parents who see our role as parents being intertwined with and dependent upon our first role as people.

I read these essays and write new ones to remind me of many experiences and lessons. Now I see how silly I am sometimes, both as a parent and as a person. They remind me of how ironic it is that we're given babies who need only holding, loving, and basic physical care at a time when we think we have so many answers—and later can offer only holding and loving to teenagers who want the answers we lost long ago. I now understand and accept the tender yet sad truth that the generations love each other but have little ability to listen to or learn from each other, and so they insist on repeating the other's errors.

Most of all, I realize people learn from their own experiences and having children is a gold mine of experience. My children are a large part of my life—a frustrating, funny, loving, sometimes ugly, but always challenging part of my life—but they aren't my whole life. I can't hold on to them as my reason for being. I can't move with them through their lives any more than I could have squeezed beside them into their kindergarten desks. They've touched my life and forced me to grow. We've watched and helped each other be slowly born into what we are today and what we will become tomorrow. That's the best people who love each other can do.

If I could begin again and parent each of my children

from infancy onward, I would be better because I am stronger and more confident. But instead, I'm faced with completely new experiences with my seventeen-year-old daughter, my sixteen-year-old son, and my thirteen-year-old son. Having gone through a particular age with one or two children is no help since each is unique. So I muddle through.

I try to pull some wisdom from my years of experience to deal with new situations—whether they be joyful or sorrowful—but the wisdom is rarely there. Instead, I'm comforted by my acceptance of good intentions and the reminder that I'm less than perfect. My role as parent gives me more satisfaction now because I respect my attempts to encourage and nurture my children. My mistakes are forgiven. I'm growing. I'm better than I used to be. I'm doing the best I can.

I'm Going To Write A Book

Feeling the need to be perfect to ensure we'll be loved is as familiar as the robin's whistle heralding spring.
—Karen Casey

Perfectionism is an iron cocoon wrapped protectively around weakness and fear. It provides safety, but unlike the silken coverings from which butterflies emerge, this cocoon's metal bands unnaturally restrict the being within. Perfectionism's only function is to protect by isolation; it doesn't allow those most necessary elements of human development—openness, growth, and change.

I lived safely in this manner for over thirty years. How happily these years were lived really doesn't matter to a perfectionist; safety is everything. Those years were spent in building a bigger and better cocoon—doing only those things I did well, never taking risks, rarely daring to try new things. I worked to "look" good, to cleverly entertain others with my wit, and to be loved by everyone. The exterior I created was a marvel to see; the interior was a fragile child, forever looking for acceptance and approval from "big" people.

Circumstances forced me, from time to time, to pry open a wedge in my cocoon and tentatively venture forth with no protection for my vulnerable psyche. Most often, the light was too bright or the danger too great, and I hastily retreated to safety. Parenting, however, stripped me of the option of retreat. The intensity of a parent-child relationship and my children's need for honesty have forced me into the glaring light of day. All my warts, moles, and character defects stand center stage for all to see. And just in case a passerby might miss them, my children stand ever ready to point them out.

5

I miss the old cocoon sometimes, because not all of the things I feared were imaginary. Risk exposes me to embarrassment and failure, and I've learned well the meaning of both. Openness invites rejection. Attempts to grow frequently result in frustration. I'm not always safe, and I'm not always loved. Even my children, who love me, don't always love me, and they've clearly said that more than a few times. The temptation is always there to crawl back into that snug perfectionism whenever I feel unloved or alone or afraid.

Never was that temptation so strong as when my proposal for this book was accepted. My initial exhilaration soon transformed into an almost overwhelming fear. What if people read my book? They'd know how vulnerable and unsure of myself I am. They'd see the chaos I sometimes try to pass off as normal family life. They might think I'm a bad mother.

I may have ducked into the cocoon briefly; I wrote several glib essays about a cutesy family with a loving father and mother and three adorable children. Gradually, through the months of writing, that supposed all-American family gave way on paper to a more accurate family portrait, primarily because, as I wrote, the truth of our day-to-day family life constantly mocked the candy-coated, everything's-dandy family I tried to create. The pink-cheeked "paper dolls" were drab in comparison to the three vibrant youngsters who impatiently demanded meals and some semblance of motherly care. The Robert Young father paled beside the authentic man who tried to squeeze some fatherly attention into a schedule that included a 50-hour work week, night meetings, and an attempt to launch a new business.

I was saddened to have to set aside the motherly me I'd written about in those first essays; she was the person I'd longed to be, the one I'd pretended for a long time to be. She had desserts and cookies in the freezer awaiting unexpected company. Her home, though comfortable and lived in, could accommodate emergency surgery with no danger of infection. She wore a scarf around her hair when she washed windows. I think she owned an apron and ironed dish towels. I began missing her the moment I began describing myself truthfully—a mother and wife whose family could leave notes on the dusty TV screen, one who has not one cookie recipe memorized, a woman whose family has seen only her back in the months she sat writing a book. My children have come to me as I wrote, asking a question or permission to do this or that, and my stock answer—only half-jokingly—has been, "Leave me alone; I'm writing about being a mother." Several times this summer, I suddenly became aware of being alone in the house. A pang of fear hit me: Where were my children? Then, like an old tape recorder playing in my ears, I could vaguely hear their voices asking or telling me about their plan; I could faintly remember saying yes, but often I couldn't remember what I'd said yes to.

"I'm going to write a book," I'd told them last winter, and they all had been enthusiastic and happy for me. "About parenting," I'd added, and their responses became guarded. They've seen what I've written, and in a few cases when I thought what I'd written was more about them than me, I'd asked their permission. Usually they said yes, but even the occasional no became a yes after they thought about it. I understood their hesitation. It's not easy to be open especially about mistakes or raw emotions like anger. They've lived in their own cocoons from time to time, but I hope they've never withdrawn into perfectionism out of fear of not being loved. I can sympathize with them as they vacillate between needing to be open and wanting to be safe, between having pride in their accomplishments and being disappointed that they can't do more. It's the same principle at work in my life as I rejoice in the opportunity to write a book and wish at the same time that I owned an apron.

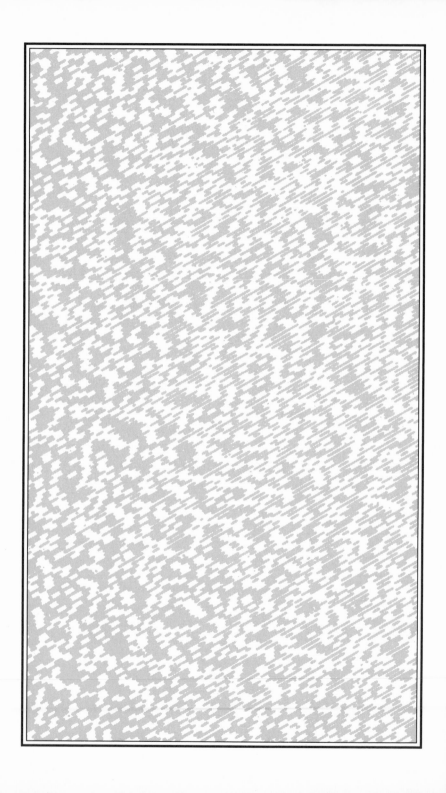

Confidence

How fortune brings to earth the oversure.

—*Petrarch*

I never doubted my qualifications for being a good parent. My qualities were impeccable—patience, honesty, a capacity for love, kindness, all of the Boy Scout oath, and a substantial part of the Sermon on the Mount. I was ready. Lucky would be the children who won me in the parent lottery!

This confidence sustained me for many years into adulthood, until one day when I was 28. The hospital staff plopped my three-day-old child into my arms, plunked me into a wheelchair, and taxied me out the door to where my husband waited beaming a confident good-parent grin. He gently helped me into the car, closed the door by pushing it shut to avoid slamming it, and scampered around to the driver's side. I looked down at the sleeping baby. It was a special moment and I remember it clearly. It was the last time I felt confident.

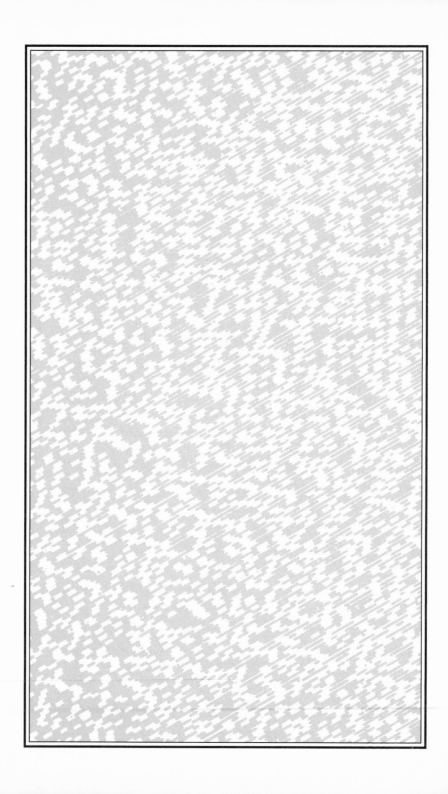

The Gifts
Unasked For

Be careful what you pray for; you may get it.

—*Anonymous*

I asked for three children. I was given three children. And the fact that I wasn't given the three I asked for has never been a disappointment to me.

The children I saw in my dreams of parenthood were perfect. They frolicked in meadows, laughing, and playing the perfect games of childhood. Their clothes were color-coordinated. The children I imagined were lovely and porcelain, nicely mannered, and stayed where I put them. The ones I was given are unmatched—not a set at all. They demanded night feedings for the first ten months of their lives. They resisted gentle play in the grass, preferring mud holes, doghouses, and dusty roads.

My dreams of marriage and children were mere extensions of the playacting from my childhood. They were "bungalow" dreams in which I'd always have bright, fluffy towels; crisp curtains; a husband who worshiped me; no financial worries; and children with perfect names like Ashley, Trenton, or Constance. I'd own a hostess gown and would entertain with flair. No chipped dishes for me, no tacky furniture.

This is what I asked for; what I was given was...well, I'm not quite sure, but certainly not what I asked for. I've been married for twenty years, and many of the towels we use were wedding gifts. My husband and I work at our marriage within a home of buzzing washers and dryers, conflicting schedules, a house crying for repair, a hodgepodge of furniture, too many bills, and too little time. And the children we were given fit right in.

These flesh-and-blood children are the gifts I never

asked for. The doll-like creatures I'd once envisioned were the playthings of a young girl or woman. They were toys to manipulate and to show off. Rather than a collection of dolls staring blankly back at me, I have three vibrant offspring who challenge, defy, and love me. They change from day to day, and I am privileged to witness and be part of their growth. Some wisdom greater than mine understands that children have their own purpose, not their parents'; so I have been given, not some cold pieces of porcelain perfection, but instead three children who pulse with their own needs, strengths, and weaknesses. When they spontaneously throw their arms around me, they are warm and sincere. They're my children. They are real.

Then And Now

A man travels the world over in
search of what he needs and returns
home to find it.

—*George Moore*

My hometown was small, a village really. Our graduating class was more like a large family—a sometimes squabbling, but loyal group. We knew each others' birthdays and middle names. We knew each others' parents and grandparents and would greet them whenever and wherever we saw them.

With a population of 650, the town had few secrets. Affairs or inconvenient pregnancies were as quickly known as last night's football score. It wasn't as if the people of my youth were cruel; it was just a small-town fact of life—everyone was aware of the smallest events in the others' lives, and they discussed them.

Young people, perhaps more than older people, need privacy, and there was very little of that when I was growing up. The escapades, failures, and misjudgments of young people were especially juicy items of discussion on Main Street, and it seemed as though we were constantly observed, gossiped about, and squealed on by people whose youth, at best, was only a dim recollection. If I drove too fast in town or honked my horn to express my youthful exuberance, I was identified immediately by people who not only knew my birth date and middle name, but also the make and model of my father's car. By the time I came home from school the next day, my parents knew every move I'd made the night before.

My mother would meet me at the door with "Mrs. Nosejoint called today."

Following the first rule of teenagedom, I'd feign deafness and force her to repeat her sentence.

"Mrs. Nosejoint called today," Mom would say more loudly.

"Oh, who's she?" (Second rule: Never admit to knowing the accuser.)

"You know her. She lives next door to Jim Eyefuls. The white house east of them. She's the one who brought the azalea when Grandma was in the hospital. You know."

"Oh, yeah. I remember her. How is she?"

"She's fine, but she asked if you were in town last night because she thought she saw our car going through town pretty fast. Even honked in front of their house."

The discussion from this point was all downhill. I'd finally admit to *maybe* driving a little too fast one time, but the real issue to me was the unfairness of being spied on. I had no privacy, nor did any of my friends. Our lives were spent in the cliched fishbowl surrounded by wrinkled faces pressing against the glass to get a closer look. They analyzed me and discussed me. Nearly every reference to me included my family tree: "You know her. She's Henry Nelson's granddaughter. Her grandma's a Larsen. Live north of the Jensens. They rent that quarter section from the Doctor's widow." And on. And on. No secrets. No place for a young person's privacy. I lived there for seventeen years and then escaped to college and eventually to an exciting city.

It's almost 30 years since I left my hometown. Ironically, I live happily in a small town with my husband and our children. Admittedly, the 30 years have brought many changes to me, but I see even more change in small-town living. For whatever reasons—the greater openness of our society, the increased mobility, or the breakdown of the traditional family and community functions—the gossip is gone. Oh, there are some small exchanges such as about business places opening up, marriages and divorces, and police scanner information, but the gossip that stripped people of their privacy is gone. There is peace and quiet—one of the reasons we choose small-town living—and only rarely are we disturbed on our secluded side street by screeching tires. Our neighbors are gentle, kind people who water our garden and pick up our newspapers when we are gone for a few days. Although this town is somewhat larger than my hometown, I find that I do know quite a few people and even a simple trip to the grocery store gives me a chance to visit with friends and acquaintances.

I know my children's friends and, in many cases, their families, and I'm warmed by their greetings when we run into each other. I think they sense my interest in them; they seem to enjoy our chance visits. Many of these youngsters are dating, driving, and holding jobs, and it seems only yesterday that they were playing tag and capture the flag in our backyard. I guarded over them then as though they were mine and was secure in knowing that when my children were playing elsewhere another concerned parent was watching and protecting them.

That security is still here as my children go through their teens. I would guess they sense the loving interest the townspeople have in them, just as I try to let their friends see my concern in their growth and welfare. I hope they do. The feeling of safety and security is, after all, the primary reason we felt that a small town was an ideal place to raise our children.

The Cold,
Cruel World

*The essence of being human is that
one does not seek perfection.*
            —George Orwell

My babies were perfect. Besides having the correct number of fingers and toes and developing physically and mentally in perfect time to what the baby manual described as normal, they all were specially blessed with a trusting nature and an openness that embraced everyone around them. They joyously responded to everyone near them, volunteering smiles, hugs, and love. Although I delighted in their perfection, I was also burdened by it. As their parent, I felt compelled to protect them from the cruelty of the world.

Thinking back on those new-baby years, I'm embarrassed by my ignorance of human nature. My attitude toward my children, and my belief in their perfection, were similar to my earliest struggles with religious thought. After my Sunday school class studied the Garden of Eden story, I refused to eat apples, thinking that I could return to a state of perfection after cleansing myself of the evil fruit. That the word *apple* never appears in this Bible story was a stunning revelation to me years later, as were the concepts of original sin and the imperfectness of human beings. But long before this understanding, I had abandoned my apple-free diet, possibly because of an innate sense of my own weakness, but more likely due to my mother's apple strudel. In both of these cases—the innocence of babies and the Garden of Eden fruit—I had foolishly viewed people as basically perfect and capable of remaining (or again becoming) perfect if only they could

17

be protected from corrupting influences.

Practical experience in parenting gradually forced me to see my perfect children more realistically. Faced with a choice between personally accepting responsibility for all their less-than-perfect behaviors or accepting that they (and I) are less-than-perfect, I opted for the latter. Oh, I'm willing to carry a measure of guilt for my parenting sins of commission and omission—sometimes, in fact, I'm more willing to do this than to glory in my successes—but I see my children more clearly now. They are not perfect treasures to be protected from a flawed world; they are valuable human beings whose strengths will better the world and whose flaws give them opportunity for growth.

The changes in my attitude toward my children have influenced how I see the world. Before, when I hovered protectively like a she-tiger pacing around her young, I saw and heard threats in every corner and was prepared to claw out in defense of my children's vulnerability. Now, the world looks less threatening, and my children, less vulnerable. It's not a matter of "them" and "us." Our home is merely a microcosm of a larger unit to which it belongs; we struggle with the same fears, disappointments, pains, and frustrations and rejoice in the same triumphs, love, and kindness as the world at large. I no longer fear the time—only a short distance ahead—when I must send my children into a cold, cruel world. Instead, I welcome the time when they will respond to an awaiting world, a world away from me and one for which they are ready.

The Ice Skates

Everywhere, we learn only from those whom we love.

—*Goethe*

She pursed her lips and squinted in concentrated effort as she carefully laced her new skates. Although they were an asked-for gift, we hadn't realized how much she wanted to learn to skate until she got them. As soon as she'd opened the gift, she had begun wheedling her parents to take her to the rink. Her excitement was evident now as she squirmed impatiently while her father tightened the laces and tied them. He lifted her over the low barrier and set her on the ice.

Her skates had barely touched the ice before she turned her head uncomfortably to her left. Immediately she curled her arms around herself. Her left arm went behind her against her lower back, and her right arm reached tightly across her stomach. She looked as though she were preparing to bow. But then, in one dramatic move—like Moses at the Red Sea—she flung her right arm up and out, followed by a similar uncoiling motion with her left arm. At the same time, she lifted her little chin and cast her eyes downward similar to the disdainful look of a ballerina. She was trying to do a pirouette! Her blissful look lasted only a split second before she fell on her bottom. Surprise and disappointment were spelled across her face. She refused to skate again that year.

My daughter's expectations were understandable. A five year old watching skating championships on TV is deceived by the grace of those athletes. What fun! How easy! she must have thought as she fantasized herself gliding and spinning across the ice. Such dreams and fantasy are the essence of youth.

I began as a parent with similar fantasies—what fun, how easy to put on the garb of a parent and then perform. I fully expected to be of Olympian status without ever going through the junior ranks. Like her, I had watched the graceful performances of others, but had never thought about years of practice, training, or even natural ability. Like her, I strapped on my gear and stepped out confidently, prepared to dazzle. But unlike her, I couldn't opt to postpone or quit when fantasy turned to hard truth.

So I practice and train as a parent. Some moves are easier for me; some I don't think I'll ever get the hang of. I ask for advice from more experienced parents, but mostly I practice and train. I move with greater ease now; sometimes I even manage a small spin—nothing fancy, but a spin nevertheless. At times, when the ice is smooth and few obstacles or people block my way, I'm able to glide and turn with confidence. Such maneuvers no doubt impress the less experienced onlookers as I sweep by them, and I like the look of respect I see on their faces. My joy is diminished only by the humbling knowledge that as soon as I've flown by them, they'll be able to see the snow on my backside.

Letting Go

There is, of course, a difference between what one seizes and what one possesses.

—*Pearl S. Buck*

The strings twisted about my hand tighten as the red, yellow, and blue balloons at their ends pull and tug to be free. I barely notice the discomfort. I'm aware, instead, of admiring glances from passersby as my children and I walk through the fairgrounds. *We're like a picture,* I think. *A mother and her children at the fair.* Her children. So possessive. It sounds as if I own them. Sometimes I feel as if I do, as if I've bought and paid for them with both financial and emotional investment. But I know they don't feel owned. They believe they are free, and they pull away and howl with protest whenever I remind them of my ownership.

But now they are getting tired. It's been a long day, too long for them and too long for a mother to "do" the fair with a two, four, and six year old. They begin to whine and pull at me; the younger two want to be held, as does the older one who thinks she's too old to admit it. I pick up the baby and offer my hands as best I can to the others, but the balloons batter me in the face. I decide quickly and say to the children, "Watch." Lifting my arm skyward, I rotate my hand to unwind the strings, and first one, then the other two balloons shoot skyward. The wind lifts them in a rocking motion, and we "ooooh" as one balloon narrowly misses being ensnarled in a tree. Soon they are small dark pinpoints against the sky, and but for the deep marks on my hand where the strings once were, it is hard to believe they were ever within my grasp. I hoist the two year old onto my hip and hold him in place with the side of my elbow while offering that outturned hand to my older son; my daughter takes my other hand. They hold tightly to me as I take my children home.

Home Is Where
The Work Is

A house is a machine for living in.
—Le Corbusier
(Charles Edouard Jeanneret)

A house has been many things to me—a ball and chain, a status symbol, an embarrassment, a financial strain, a shrine. All of these have one common element—they're burdensome. They pull on me, drain me, and demand more of me. The house's need for repair and maintenance and my need to show and impress have combined to make me a monster who (1) carps and complains because no one else helps maintain the ball and chain or (2) scolds and reprimands because other family members are not suitably respectful of the shrine I've uncovered under the dust.

To think of a house as a machine changes my attitude. Instead of being a burden to be served and cared for, my home is a physical object constructed for the sole purpose of serving our needs. We need shelter, and the house provides shelter. We require a place to gather as a family, and the house is here for us. Privacy is necessary, and the walls are constructed to isolate us from the world when we wish. We can add beauty to our lives in the furnishings we select for our home. The house is there for us, not we for the house. Thinking this way helps free me of a home's supposed demands. I see this structure more clearly as a machine we've purchased to fulfill our needs. If it looks lived in, so be it; it's only a machine. The people and the activities within these walls are my most important consideration, and, given a choice, I will invest my energies into them and ignore the groans, whines, and complaints of an abused machine.

The Danger
Of Daring

*Avoiding danger is no safer in the long
run than outright exposure. The fearful
are caught as often as the bold.*
—Helen Keller

"Oh, be careful." I've said this...how many
times? More than dozens. Certainly hundreds. And maybe even thousands of times.
My children recognized these words before "Mommy"
and "Daddy." These were the first words they learned
to ignore, followed closely by "no." My toddlers were
cautioned from the moment they first wobbled on their
newly found legs. Unmindful of my warnings, they
proceeded to gleefully fling themselves into walls, cupboard doors, and table edges. Our house became a giant
pinball machine; my children, like balls, bounced from
one bumper to another, lighting lights, setting off buzzers
and my ringing cry of "Be careful." Despite my
vigilance, two of them disappeared down the penalty
hole (the basement steps), only to pop back up and roll
into play again. Occasionally they did get hurt—nothing
life threatening, but frightening or painful enough to
send them to my arms for a moment of comfort or first
aid. Then, off they went again, looking for furniture to
damage with their heads.

I've be-carefulled my children so perfectly that I no
longer realize I'm saying the words; like a "Bless you"
to a sneeze, the "Be careful" is a nonthinking, patterned
reflex to every imagined threat to my children's safety.
Swimming, bike riding, wrestling, wood burning—it
doesn't matter what the activity is—all require, for my
sense of peace, a called-out "Be careful." That it's said
instinctively or that it's unheard, matters not at all; I continue to say it.

Examining my motives isn't a big day brightener for me, for they are less than honorable. I know my words don't change in the least what my children do or how they do it. Certainly, only a fool would expect a youngster to think, *oh, look how fast I'm driving, and Mom did tell me to be careful. I'll just ease up on the speed so I don't get hurt. Lucky for me that Mom reminded me of this. Or, Mom told me to be careful, so instead of jumping from this limb, I'm going to inch my way back down the tree. I probably would have broken a bone if she hadn't warned me.* I'm not a fool; I have no delusions that my sons or daughter even think of me or my cautions as they careen through their days and nights.

What I am, is afraid—superstitiously afraid they will get hurt if I don't say the magic words and, even more difficult to admit, selfishly afraid that if evil does befall them, it would be my fault. So I warn them to ward off any chance of being accountable, of feeling guilty. The logical extension of this reasoning would be hilarious if it weren't so tragic. Imagine being contacted by a law or medical official with gory details of a child's accident and absolving self-guilt by saying, "Oh, no, I *told* them to be careful."

I'm uncomfortable with this new understanding of my cautiousness. I've believed my actions and words to spring from mature, conscientious parenting, not from a childish need to be good or right. Like so many of my analytical excursions into parenting, this one leaves me empty and sad. Another similarity, however, gives me hope. Almost every time I really think about my children and one of their behaviors that bothers me, I end up seeing myself more clearly. That clarity gives me a place to begin a better life and, hopefully, better parenting.

Now, instead of trying to decide how to encourage more caution in my children, I'm working to rid myself of unreasonable fear. Fear of being wrong, of being hurt, has stripped my life of adventure. Being unwilling to take chances has deprived me of spontaneity and of the ability to see the difference between large and small risks. Certainly, I don't intend to foolishly expose myself to near-certain physical dangers or even emotional hurts. As has been so often true, I can learn from my children and imitate their healthy attitudes toward new and unknown things. More of my regrets center on things I didn't do than on those I did. I can't go back and accept past challenges to see if I will succeed or fail; now I'll never know. But I do have the remainder of my life to experiment with. I can take chances if I allow myself to be wrong or hurt or disappointed. My children are good models for the behavior I want for my own. Like them, I can be unafraid and hurl myself headlong into the adventure of living with no guarantees and no protective headgear.

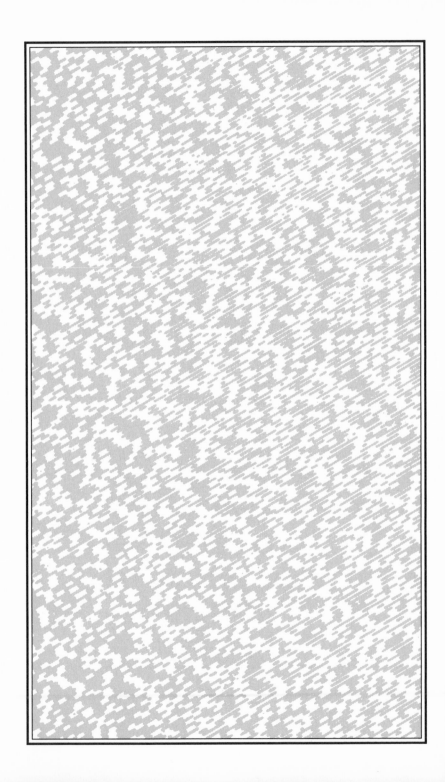

A Child's Coming
And Going

*A child's nature is too serious a thing
to admit of its being regarded as a
mere appendage of another being.*
—Charles Lamb

Sometimes a feeling much like mourning engulfs me when I look through the mementos of my children's early years. A lock of hair, footprints on birth records, and even the handprint plaque that hangs on our bedroom wall stir an unwelcome sense of regret or loss. Each represents a time long gone, an opportunity lost. The little boy with the white-blond curls has become a young man, no longer a dreamer—a solid, serious thinker with straight brown hair. The tiny footprints on paper seem to have no relationship to the man- and woman-size shoes lying inside the entry door. The small hand that made the plaque has not reached for the safety of mine in several years. My son made the plaque in nursery school when he was four. Taped on its back is a poem:

Sometimes you get discouraged
Because I am so small
And always leave my fingerprints
On furniture and walls.

But every day I'm growing
I'll be grown up someday
And all those tiny handprints
Will surely fade away.

So here's a final handprint
Just so you can recall
Exactly how my fingers looked
When I was very small.

29

When my thoughts wander within this sad nostalgia, I remind myself to recheck my memories. They are often distorted and romanticized by wishful thinking. If I've allowed myself to believe my children were once really mine—to believe I had been the center of their world and was all-important to them—then I am saddened by their growth. But more accurate are memories of them twisting their hands from mine so they could toddle off to explore, of them impatiently wriggling free from my lap in order to play, and of them joyously waving good-bye as they bounded off to their toy box, to the swings, to nursery school, to a friend's house.

I was important to them as a center, yes, but only as a center from which they constantly left and to which they returned. And it was no different then, when they were young, than it is now. They've grown and matured, so naturally they share with me in different ways than before. But they still do share. They leave me with longer and jauntier strides; they return more confident. But they still leave and return.

Recently, my younger son and I were shopping in a mall, and within seconds of our arrival he left me. When my shopping was finished, I walked to the pet store, our meeting place. He'd been watching for me, I could tell, because as soon as I came in, he impatiently motioned me to join him. "Mom, look at these." He stood beside a glassed-in pen; two puppies wriggled and whined within. He reached over the edge to touch them. Instantly, their little pink tongues licked the large, rough hand. He spread out his fingers, and I thought of my handprint plaque. He chuckled with pleasure and watched intently as the puppies jostled each other for control of his hand. One lost its balance and tumbled clumsily onto its side. I laughed. My son glanced up at me and beamed. Again he had returned.

Value Messages

Human life has its laws, one of which is: We must USE things and LOVE people.

—*John Powell*

Too often I give my children the wrong message about the importance of things and people. My concern over a tear in a new item of clothing says clearly, "THIS has value; you do not." Or, at the very least, it implies a greater value on the thing than on the child. Sometimes, I realize that I discipline my children differently depending on the result of their behavior. If they throw a tennis ball in the house, I merely tell them to stop. If they throw a tennis ball in the house and break a lamp, I discipline them more severely. Clearly, my emphasis is on things. In my refusal to let them use the "good" car, I might be implying that an accident would cost more to repair on the newer automobile.

I need to make clearer statements to my children about their worth. Certainly, I'm not going to make a complete reversal and allow my children to run wild, leaving mud tracks and chaos in their wake. But I can make better value judgments when faced with my great-grandmother's broken platter or a scraped right-front fender. I can more clearly tell my children that the value of things lies in their usefulness, their sentiment, and their beauty; and that we love people because they are lovable, not merely useful.

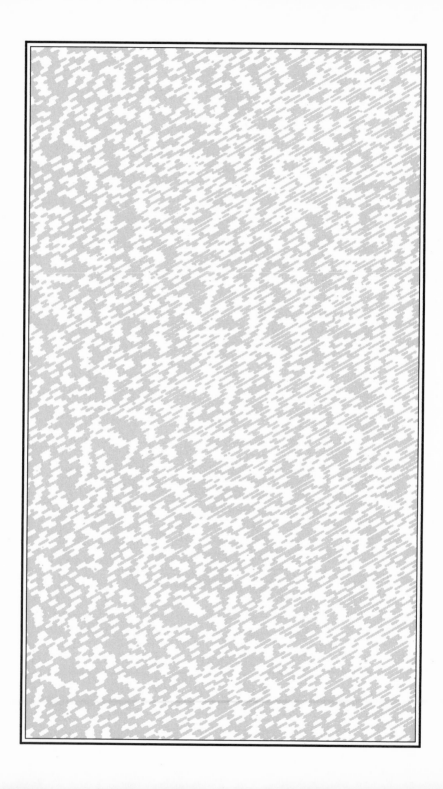

Improving Upon
My Parents

*The more things change, the more they
stay the same.*

—Alphonse Karr

My children don't wear boots, and I struggle to understand. My sons did for a time, but they soon took note of their sister's resistance to them and abandoned use of them entirely.

At first I thought I understood their dislike of boots. Some are quite bulky—serviceable, my father would have called them—and they don't fit the image projected by the trim ski jackets and warm, but lightweight, gloves that young people seem to favor.

I remember well the disgust I felt toward a pair of boots my parents once gave me and—worse yet—expected me to wear. They had buckles that looked too much like the farm boots we all had to wear into the barn and chicken house. Barb, the girl I most admired for her beauty and wonderful wardrobe, had fur-topped boots, and it was fur-topped boots that I envisioned as I opened the box that contained my "manure" boots. (I called them this only in my mind; I wouldn't have dared hurt my parents by saying it out loud.) Worse luck yet, my feet stopped growing about that time, and those serviceable boots refused to wear out until years later.

My sensitivity had been honed by that painful experience of my youth, so I was better able than my parents to understand my children's wishes. When my daughter was in ninth grade, she began to walk to the high school, about a half-mile from our house. I ached for her as she strode off in rain, snow, or slush with only shoes on her feet—thin shoes at that and often with no socks. For a month or so before Christmas, I carefully shopped for earmuffs, scarf, and boots that would complement her new winter jacket and be stylish enough to move her to wear them.

They were all maroon and perfectly matched the plaid in her ski jacket. Before wrapping them, I had secretly checked them against her jacket after she had gone to bed. On Christmas morning, the children tore into their packages. When she came to the unmistakable large package, I watched her closely. The expression on her face said it all. And all it said was disappointment. She thanked us and commented on how well they matched her jacket, but her expression clearly said "manure boots," or whatever a city girl would call them.

I'm not often gifted with a lot of insight, but that winter morning I was. I suddenly saw the irony of the situation, and it was sad, but funny. I so often think that I am so much more sensitive to my children than my parents were, that I understand them so much better than my parents understood me. But there was my daughter trying to be appreciative of a pair of boots that she knew she would rarely wear. When shopping, I had tried to see the boots through her eyes, but all I had were my own. The boots were beautiful, and they did match her winter ensemble perfectly. But in trying to delight her, I had made the same mistake my parents had made years earlier. The boots I'd given her were maroon and they were trim, but mostly they were fur-topped—they were the boots I'd wanted when I was fourteen.

The Idealist

Youth can measure in only one direction—forward, from things as they are, to their ideal of what things ought to be.

—Eric Sevareid

In this day of proclaiming slogans and beliefs on T-shirts, my children should have seven, one for every day of the week, on which is emblazoned THAT'S NOT FAIR. And my shirts would read BUT THAT'S THE WAY IT IS. This could save us considerable time. Many of our conversations could be replaced with grimaces and emphatic gestures to our chests. But instead, we just argue; they, the rightness of their cause; and I, the futility of trying to change the system.

They will come to my point of view—in time. Their innocence and idealism will be buffeted by years of reality. They will come to accept "the way it is." Realizing this makes me sad. There's a zest to their idealism, a purity, a treasure I'll miss. Their wholesome view of right and wrong and of how things should be is the essence of their youth; it is a strength of youth. And I once had it.

My children are right in many ways. Their causes are just. Just admitting that makes the gap between us smaller. They aren't wrong to protest the unmeasured dangers of nuclear power. They aren't wrong to claim a right to a world as clean as we inherited. They aren't wrong to be embarrassed when I close my eyes to political maneuverings that are dishonest or self-serving. I've been wrong to accept "the way it is" in the name of maturity. It has never been mature to accept dishonesty because it is expedient, or waste because it's profitable, or injustice because it doesn't occur in my backyard.

I've been wrong. I've snuggled down into that comfortable bed of age, claiming that things couldn't or shouldn't be changed, or that those who cry out are mistaken or misinformed. I've allowed myself to be hoodwinked by a comfortable income and to be lulled into complacency by retirement planning. I've forgotten my obligations to leave the world a better place. Perhaps I could still stretch myself and recapture a bit of that righteous indignation. So what if I can't win? The wrongs I've blinded myself to should be questioned and called to task. And other idealistic, caring people might even join me. Those people might even be my children.

All Of The Family

*Before most people start boasting
about their family tree, they usually
do a good pruning job.*
—O. A. Battista

It's so tempting to clean up all the relatives my children see and hear about. My own past and present would look much better if laundered too. The pressures of role modeling encourage me to deodorize and sanitize all my accounts of relatives I share with my kids. Uncle So-and-So could have just as well died in the war as in prison. Great-grandmother could have been a saint who dedicated her life to her family and not an unhappy young woman who abandoned the four children who, 60 years later, refused to visit her deathbed. My own father could have been a teetotaler who came home each evening for dinner and read stories to his children before bedtime. There's a certain appeal to this. I could plunge us all into hot, soapy water, follow it with a good rinse and heavy starch, and then present a rigid line of role models to my children. "And here," I could say, "are your relatives. Follow their lead and you, too, will be happy and successful."

I want to do this. I really wish life for my children could be an extension of the gentle, unthreatening world of fuzzy bunnies, carousel rides, and Mr. Rogers. But instead, we talk about the tragedy of basically good people making bad choices or of sometimes having no choice. I tell them about a man who seemed to find no place for himself in the world and died alone. About a young woman—a girl really—who could not take her children with her when she fled her abusive husband. About a man whose life choices were made by his addiction and whose family saw more anger than love.

My children live their lives, not within story books, but within the confines of their own strengths and weaknesses and the opportunities and limitations presented. As all of us do, they will have to make choices and live with the results, good or bad. I don't want to cripple them with false expectations of fairy-tale endings or of three wishes to make everything better. But equally important is their understanding that harsh choices or severe limitations don't have to crush people. Their relatives, I tell them, are no better or no worse than the rest of the world. We all have had to deal with disappointment, pain, and limitations, but we've found joy and love and satisfaction in our lives despite our mistakes and failures. This optimism of finding happiness regardless of false starts or disastrous mistakes is what I hope I have given my children.

Security Of Place

*Home is the place where, when you
have to go there,
They have to take you in.*
—Robert Frost

My sister still lives on the farm where we were raised. The house—set in the midst of rich Iowa farmland—is sturdy, stable, and virtually unchanged in twenty years. Nearby, a small creek still rises every spring, flooding a slough in the pasture and creating a hubbub of activity. Wild flowers bloom everywhere, and mallards and killdeers nest and raise their young. It's a child's dream—one in which to watch the real world and fantasize another. A child can spend hour upon hour there chasing butterflies, collecting minnows and tadpoles in coffee cans, and threatening toothpick-legged baby killdeers so that the mother will shriek and flop on the ground, as though wounded, to draw the predator away. A child can depend on the predictability of the seasons, the people, and the lifestyle there.

In contrast, my husband, I, and our three children moved yet again when our younger son was six. It was the sixth house he'd lived in, the fifth town. Looking for a house, buying, selling, and closing are facts of life for us—so much so that my husband didn't even see one house I bought until we drove by it on our way to the closing.

"Moving is exciting," I tell my children. "Don't think so much about the friends you leave behind; think about the new friends waiting for you in the new town. You'll make friends right away because we'll live in town again and you'll meet lots of kids." I'm not trying to fool them; I do believe that life is an adventure. It's filled with exciting new experiences and people that we can learn from and with whom we make a shared history.

My mother wrote to me that first September after our sixth move in June. Her letter was filled with the usual family and hometown information—who did what, who went where. Just that last week, she wrote, the tomatoes were crying to be canned, so she, my sister, and my sister-in-law worked for two days "out on the farm" putting up dozens of quarts of juice, stewed tomatoes, and sauce. She wrote only two or three lines about the canning, but the scene was so vivid. For whatever reason— her description or my memory—I clearly saw the three of them moving about the kitchen table and standing at the sink cleaning and quartering the juicy red fruits, while the kettle-laden stove in the corner steamed with tomatoes in various stages of preparation. I could feel the warm moistness of the kitchen, smell the pungent aroma, and even see through the kitchen window, beyond the pump house and barn, to the slough— withered and brown—lying idle and waiting for another spring. Overriding all this was the anxiousness, the anticipation—like footracers waiting at their mark—of another harvest season.

I cried with loneliness for "my people," for my home, for the place I owned by right of birth. I cried for my unclaimed right to be there and for being left out. Excitement and newness be damned, I thought; what about tradition, stability, and the freedom not to have to explain who you are?

When my children came home from school later that day, I greeted them with a new awareness. They might not have decades of place history or the stability of the family name on buildings or farms, but in this move they had sacrificed a greater portion of place stability than I had.

I talk differently to my children now than I once did. Some of the words are the same—life is still an adventure, and there *is* excitement in moving. We have learned to be more adaptable and flexible in meeting new people, and we are fortunate to have friends in many places. But I'm more honest with them and with myself about the flip side of being a mobile family— we will never see a tree we plant grow to any great height, they will not graduate with kindergarten classmates, and they will never be able to bike over to Grandma's after school like many of their friends do.

Parenting is an even greater responsibility for mobile families. My children have no one place they can claim other than the confines of our house and our family wherever we might be living at any given time. No people nearby knew them as babies; no one here witnessed their baptisms. For history and tradition of place, our family is all they have. Despite the love and commitment we feel toward our children, there have been many times that our family has not been enough. We haven't provided the same security of place that I once knew, that I can still know if I choose to return.

But some things are predictable, and I find comfort in them. We have established some family traditions— holiday meals, vacations and trips, and other special practices like birthday dinners that provide our children with an all-important sameness. Each spring I keep an eye out for the distinctive stilt-like gait of the killdeer. My children—who somehow understand how much I enjoy these birds and their behavior—watch for them too. When we see a mother and her military line of young, we slowly walk toward them. Closer, closer, and then suddenly the mother will cry out and fly off a short ways. The young drop deathly still to the earth, while their mother in the distance shrieks as though in pain and flops on the ground pulling her "broken" wing along the grass. We watch, fascinated, as this simple bird struggles valiantly to protect her babies from a world suddenly grown hostile, suddenly so changed.

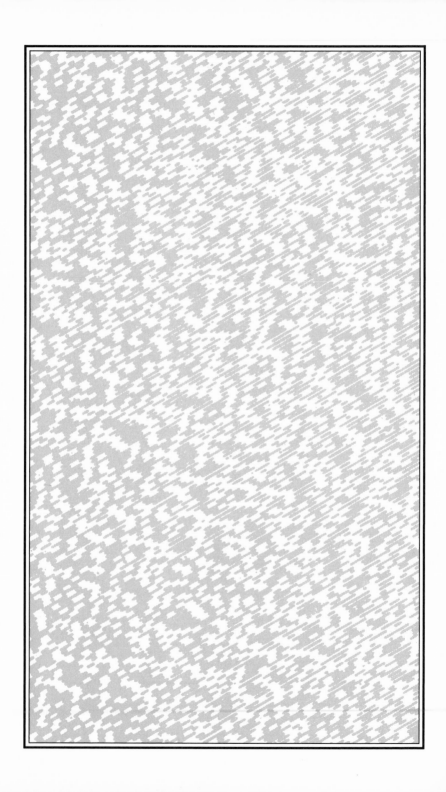

Blood, Sweat, And Cheers

The combative instinct is a savage prompting by which one man's good is found in another's evil.
—George Santayana

We encouraged our children to play in competitive sports as soon as they could lift a bat, swing a golf club, or tuck a football under an arm. I say encouraged, not pushed. There was no primitive need on my part to vicariously live through my children's participation in sports. Neither I nor my husband was like those gung-ho parents who scream and threaten from the sidelines, while their lilliputian-like clones galumph erratically across the playing surface. We emphasize that the decision to join athletics is theirs and that their decision should rest on pleasing themselves, not us.

I understand very well the joys and benefits of organized sports for children of all ages. My own experience in high school basketball and softball is at the root of that understanding. Participation in athletics affirmed me and gave me a sense of personal worth by using the physical characteristic—my height—that otherwise was a source of pain and embarrassment for me. I understand the thrill of physical challenge. I understand the satisfaction that comes with conditioning and training. I understand the growth that comes from setting personal goals and the amazement when those goals are actually achieved.

How well I understand became clear to me only recently. My son came home from a tennis match, tired but aglow with a slight sunburn and a mist of perspiration on his face. He poured himself a glass of orange juice and collapsed into a nearby chair. I looked at my young, aspiring athlete and smiled knowingly. I understood, I remembered the exhaustion and mental replays following a competition. Sitting down across the table from him, I leaned forward and eagerly said the words that bonded us as two people who understood the value of placing demands on one's body. "Well," I asked him, "did you win?"

Security Blanket

Words form the thread on which we string our experiences.

—Aldous Huxley

So many words pass between my children and me. So few of them have any depth. We communicate by their unwritten rules, the essence of which is we talk only about the events or times we share together—infancies, childhoods, lunch tickets, curfews, room cleaning, family plans, and money. My efforts to insert my childhood into our conversations or to move out of my traditional parenting role is met with a variety of reactions, the most obvious reaction being embarrassment. The first time I saw this was when I tried to play paper dolls with my daughter. She was about four and obsessed with *The Brady Bunch*. I had given her a book of Brady paper dolls, and we sat on her bed punching out the clothes. When we were done, she put one of the outfits on the Marcia doll. "Do you want me to play with you for a while?" I asked. She nodded. I picked up the Greg doll and waddled him across the bed toward her, saying deeply, "Hi, Marcia. Do you want to go listen to some records?"

She was horror-struck. She took the doll from my hand and said, "That's okay, Mommy. Let's not play." The clear-cut self-consciousness she felt was for me—I had stepped out of my parenting role, and she was embarrassed.

I understand the feeling, but understanding it doesn't mean I have to like it. How wonderful it would be if these children of mine had a genuine interest in me as a person, not just as a mother. Oh, they do listen to, and even enjoy sometimes, a few brief stories about my growing up. Their discomfort comes when they sense that I'm trying to draw a parallel between their lives and mine. If my story puts me on their level, they're embarrassed. Perhaps they find some stability in the distance we maintain. Maybe they see my attempts to bridge that distance as a middle-aged woman trying to recapture her youth.

My children would be enriched if they could allow themselves to see the total fabric of the lives of the adults around them. And eventually they will, but in the meantime they cling to the security of the small, familiar portion of each of us, much like small children stroking a well-worn corner of their favorite blanket.

The Boy Who Went To North Dakota

*We seek pitifully to convey to others
the treasures of our heart, but they
have not the power to accept them
and so we go lonely, side by side but
not together, unable to know our
fellows and unknown by them.*
—W. Somerset Maugham

She was 74; I was sixteen. Almost every Tuesday and Friday night through basketball season I walked to my granddmother's house after school. She lived in town and my going there gave me the time to get my homework done, eat, and rush back to school to play in the basketball game.

This never became routine to me, and I realize now the sense of restlessness and eagerness was due to the adrenaline surging through me in anticipation of the game. Basketball gave me an identity that nothing else did, and I marked my life in those years from season to season and—within each season—from game to game. In hindsight, I'm not sure if I was good or merely adequate; our school was small so even the merely adequate had a chance to shine. That uncertainty doesn't matter because at the time I believed—I knew—I was a talented athlete, and the cheering crowds and the after-game congratulations fed a tall, skinny girl's need to believe.

Even as I sat at my grandmother's dining room table, my mind was focused more on the upcoming game than on the algebra before me. Mentally, I could see my "man" moving with the ball, and I, like a shadow, flowing with her. Whether she moved to the left or the right, I wouldn't be faked out. I gloried in a certain split second when my opponent dribbled the ball, and I saw only the ball hitting the floor and starting to rise. It was then, a precise instant, that I knew I could move into the ball and own it. A little too early meant missing it and giving the opponent an open shot; a bit late meant a foul. But timed just right, the ball could be mine, and this always surprised my opponents. I loved that moment just before the ball was mine, when my opponent still thought it was hers.

I was startled from my thoughts by my grandmother's laugh. She was standing right beside me, chuckling and evidently expecting me to laugh too. I closed my book.

"I'm sorry, Grandma, but I didn't hear you. I was doing my algebra. What did you say?"

She wiped her hands on the ever-present apron which was grimy across her protruding middle. "I said," she moved her beaming face from side to side as though trying to shake the laughter from her head so she could speak, "that when my boyfriend begged me to take him back or else he'd kill himself, my mother told me that barking dogs never bite. And she was right!"

I smiled uncomfortably. Obviously, Grandma had been talking to me from the kitchen for some time while I was daydreaming, but my experience with Grandma's stories told me I'd probably not missed much. I always felt embarrassed for her when she confided in me about some long ago event. Now, here she stood—in her laced black shoes, baggy brown cotton stockings, and her arms sagging from the sleeves of her housedress—talking to me about some prehistoric boyfriend! When I was younger, I had watched my grandmother as she and my mother visited in the living room, trying to reconcile the reality of this old woman with the large wall portrait of a beautiful newlywed. I had wondered why she didn't remove the photo so others wouldn't pity her.

She laughed again, and the weathered folds beneath her jaw vibrated. I marveled at how her eyelashes could support the sagging lids that filled the curl of those lashes. I ached in embarrassment for her and wished she wouldn't insist on talking about her youth.

"The fool," she continued as she gathered and repinned the hairs shaken loose from her bun, "after he went out with that other girl, he should have known I wouldn't marry him and live on that homestead of his in North Dakota."

I suddenly laughed. "Homestead! You're kidding! You lived when people had homesteads!" I howled. My grandmother's face became hard, and I realized that in my glee I was pointing and moving my finger up and down through the air in a circling motion toward her. She had instantly understood the reason for my mirth. I hadn't joined her in her story; I was laughing at her— an old woman telling foolish stories of her youth.

"Grandma —" my voice was softened by the need to take the hurt away, but she sighed and walked back to the kitchen.

We ate a quiet meal, she with her thoughts and I thinking of outjumping a taller, thicker girl; of leading my teammate with a precision pass; of knowing the right instant to move into the ball.

My grandmother died when I was 24. She never saw me play basketball, and I never asked her about the boy who went to North Dakota.

Winning And Losing

A simple caress has the potential of changing a whole life.

—*Leo Buscaglia*

My daughter and I stood toe to toe. I repeatedly and ever more loudly refused her request; she, in matching decibels, plunged into belligerence. This had become our pattern, and I felt helpless to change it. I knew I looked foolish, screaming and claiming my right to be obeyed. And she looked like a stranger. Her eyes were steely in defiance; I was losing my power over her. It was a contest, and I was determined to win.

"Do you know what you need?" My voice was cold.

"Yeah, I guess." Her tone told me she was prepared to lose again. My threats would again save my power! But in that instant, I saw her as she was—a little girl, only twelve, who was trying to stake out a bit of property, a small chunk of herself free of me. I still didn't want to lose, but I didn't want to win either. She was so close; I put my arms around her. "I think you need a hug," I said as I nuzzled the top of her head. The embrace I received in turn told me I was indeed a wise mother. I wish I could be blessed with such wisdom more often.

Family
Consumerism

Everything which is properly business we must keep carefully separate from life.

—*Goethe*

At this moment I have a closer, more meaningful relationship with my grocer than I do with my children. He smiles when he sees me and makes me feel welcome. Sometimes we even visit in his store, exchanging nonthreatening information about family, the weather, and the price of meat. We don't look for hidden meanings in the other's words, nor do we squabble over unintended slights. Our relationship is stable, mutually productive, and healthy. In contrast, living with my children often makes me feel like I'm trying to juggle three beach balls while treading water—during a hurricane yet. I think I'm drowning.

I had once imagined raising children to be much like the marketplace. We—my children and I—would have complementary needs and services, and the process of living within a family would be the exchange of these commodities. Love, nurturing, security, and encouragement would be attractively displayed and available to all, the only costs being responsibility and loyalty to the family. Ah, those were my simplistic days when I had an answer for everything. It was at that time, too, that I knew a happy marriage depended on a balanced budget, lacy curtains, and knowing which one takes out the garbage.

The reality of marriage and raising children has humbled me and altered my smug expectations. My seventeen-year-old daughter has recently begun saying "Well, it's my life!" She has told us outright that she wants to be more free like her friends who, she claims, never have to ask parental permission. She tells me I am trying to keep her a little girl. My older son, sixteen, is a black-and-white, need-to-be-right boy who struggles to balance these traits with a desire to please the people around him. He's a perfectionist whose behavior improves when we criticize one of the other children. He's the child who is making me pay for my own upbringing; he argues and disputes the minutest details trying to prove he's right. His first words were "I know." I deserve him. My younger son is very bright. He taught himself to read when he was four, writes his own books, and creates marvelous projects for himself. The ringing phone has become my enemy, for he has invented uncounted ways in which to irritate teachers and delight classmates.

It's sad to admit, but there's also a relief in admitting it: family life is not a marketplace. If we approach our family with a shopping list in hand, we're going to be very disappointed because this little cluster of loving, but flawed, people is not a supermarket with a complete array of goods. At best, it's a mom-and-pop store with a limited inventory. We carry the major items—love and hugs, personal interest, concern, support, and good intentions. Mostly good intentions.

I don't always have what my children need, and often neither they nor I know even what it is they're shopping for. My simple answers to raising children were buried long ago under the complications of family life. Now I sometimes have complex answers; usually I have no answers at all. And how can I? Parenthood didn't miraculously form me into a finished product. I'm still growing, changing, and learning.

There is a relief in seeing myself more clearly and accepting my parenting as being the best I can do. Rewards and joys abound in a household with children, but they're not what I expected so many years ago. No day is exactly like the one before, but then, how could it be when all five of us are constantly growing and moving ahead? I hope there is a steadying balance between the highs—an unsolicited hug, a peaceful evening together, family trips, a word of praise, laughter—and the lows—who took whose shirt, what isn't fair, why's it always me, and a man and woman who have too little time together.

The reality of the difference between what I expected and what really is has been freeing because it allows— no, commands—me to see myself as a person first and as a mother second. In doing so, I've discovered that my parenting skills have been improved only by learning better living skills. I can't focus only on parenting to find my purpose in life. Now I do more things just for myself. I read. I write. I reflect. And I go grocery shopping often.

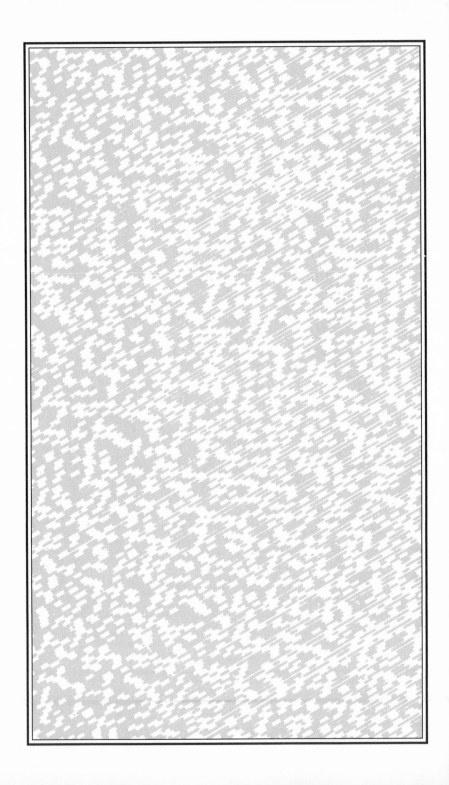

The Pathway

You are the bows from which your children as living arrows are sent forth.

—*Kahlil Gibran*

I've mistakenly pictured my children and me on a journey together. The picture is of a parent and child, hand in hand, joyously exploring a pathway. The parent patiently teaches and encourages the child's curiosity, and the child holds tightly to the larger hand and gazes up at the parent with attentive and appreciative eyes.

Of course, this is a foolish, distorted view of what parenting is actually like. A more accurate picture is of the child running blindly ahead, bony knees wildly propelling a yet-uncoordinated body into the unknown. The parent, helplessly and fearfully, calls out, "Come back! Wait for me! There might be bears!" As though sensing the longer pathway that awaits, the child waves an impatient hand and disappears over a far hill.

I must remember that my children and I do not travel this lifetime together. My responsibility is to provide them a map, a lunch for the way, and salve for bear scratches.

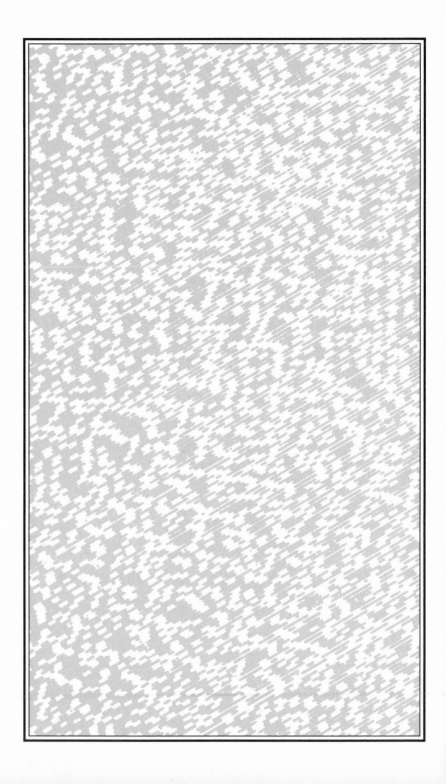

"Because" Is
An Answer

*If your heart is quite set upon a
crown, make and put on one of roses,
for it will make the prettier appearance.*
—*Epictetus*

I didn't set out to be a dictator in my own home.
Quite the contrary. The marriage and children I
planned provided a clear role for me to play: a gentle, settling presence for my family as they faced an un-
gentle, unsettling world. Rosy-cheeked sons and
daughters would listen keenly to my soft-spoken answers
to questions and requests. The power, the authority of
parenthood wasn't ignored, but I intended to wear that
authority more like a flower-bedecked hat than as an
awe-inspiring crown.

At first it was easy; I used the same good-fairy voice
to answer their questions and to explain the details of
life as I did when I read to them from their Golden
Books. But the voice got tired, mainly from overuse.
They kept asking questions and more questions, and,
as time went on, they seemed less and less satisfied with
what I had to say. Soon I began to sense a pattern in
all this. They would ask a question. I would explain
patiently. They would ask, "But why?. . ." and I would
explain some more. "But why?" Explanation. "Why?"
Explanation. Their "whys" became more whining while
my gentleness gave way to a heavier, measured voice.

Recently, our younger son turned thirteen; the three
children are teenagers, and my parenting pattern is
securely in place. Each day I arise and I figuratively put
upon my head, as I have done each morning for seventeen years, my symbol of parenthood—a garland of flowers. I approach my children with the tenderness and
kindness that I had imagined so long ago. Our pattern

carries us through our days. They ask questions or permission. I answer them, and if the answer is no, I explain. They say, "Why?" I explain. They become sullen and demand to know why. I patiently explain.

What's really going on? These children aren't asking for an answer, unless the answer is yes. It's then that I say, "For the last time, the answer is no, and we'll discuss it no more." It always saddens me if I see they aren't going to quit, because that always means a greater loss for me than for them. If they continue (and at this point they usually do), I suddenly feel foolish, standing there trying to talk reasonably and gently to someone who no longer is debating, but is attacking personality—mine. "You don't care. You never listen. Now you're mad and won't even tell me why I can't." It's then that I sense myself thrusting the flowers from my hair and dramatically replacing them with a giant crown of power. My face contorts, and my voice—no longer gentle—screeches out, "BECAUSE! Because I say so!"

Generally, this is the end of the confrontation—the end of the discussion anyway—as my child resolutely turns on heel and disappears behind a door that suddenly swings freely. I'm left feeling empty and wondering if I could have headed off this argument. Could I have said something earlier that would have made sense to my child? Probably not, since the real issue had been power, or winning, not logic. Should I have said yes to the request? I'm usually satisfied that my refusal was correct. The overall sadness I feel is caused by my anger or, more correctly, my using anger to settle the dispute. The angry queen is not caring. She's not reasonable. She's not gentle. And she's certainly not pretty.

Hot Lunch,
Cold Lunch

> *To hold the same views at forty as we held at twenty is to have been stupified for a score of years and to take rank, not as a prophet, but as an unteachable brat.*
> —*Robert Louis Stevenson*

The longer I'm a parent, the more clearly I see the paradoxes, ironies, and downright contradictions in my role. Most of these conflicting elements are due to or caused by my children. Their pains and joys force me into reflective growth, but their apparent need for me not to change is constantly fighting against that very growth. My children's sincerity and sense of rightness have renewed within me a need to take stands, speak my mind, and make a difference; but my sons and daughter have repeatedly discouraged this for reasons they've never discussed but which I suspect to be largely embarrassment.

Being a parent has made me more understanding of our human fears and weaknesses, yet my children are often angered by my attempts to help them see a conflict from the other person's perspective. When they've been hurt by one of their friends, I talk to them about how the friend might be suffering, but all they want is comfort and blind loyalty to their views. "Why do you always do that?" my older son once demanded. "Do what?" I asked. "You always say, 'But look at it from his side' or 'Think of how unhappy he must be.' And I don't want to. And I don't want you to, either."

My changing threatens them, their security, and sometimes their sense of fairness. Fairness was the issue when my older two children found out about their younger brother's cold lunch. "But that's not fair," they screeched in unison. Their reaction really surprised me, because

I had begun to let them bring cold lunches to school too. How could this possibly be unfair? They explained this to me with as much outrage as if I'd disinherited them. Fairness, they said, was the issue. "It's not fair," said my daughter, "to let him bring a cold lunch. He's only in first grade. We had to eat hot lunches until we were in fourth and fifth grade."

I wanted this to end happily, so I spent considerable time explaining to them that I had a right to change my mind. And I told them that the most important thing was to act on that change. Unfairness would be my continuing to do something that I now considered unnecessary or wrong. Repapering a living room takes less time than this conversation did. In fact, wallpapering is a joy in comparison because you know when you're done; you come to the corner where you started and presto! you're finished. This discussion went on and on. It never was finished; it continues to this day.

Now, whenever they catch me in yet another betrayal of change, they use sentences beginning with "And then there was the time..." They indignantly itemize my inconsistencies—from the time I capriciously changed their bedtimes to my sudden refusal to drive them to school, from my vindictive decision not to allow them to eat in the living room to the whimsical dictate that they had to shoulder more of the housekeeping responsibilities. And always among their long, rambling list is the unfairness of changing the no-cold-lunch rule.

It would be easier sometimes not to change. The iron-clad parenting style of my young-mother years didn't demand as much of me as the one I operate with now. Yes was Yes; No was No. And I *never* rethought, reconsidered, or—heaven forbid—changed my mind. Believing that children needed consistency and knowing that I needed to be in charge, I parented my children with an unwavering and sometimes heavy hand.

It was much easier to be a dictator than the more open

and willing-to-change parent I've become. It was also more boring, stifling, and lonely. Perhaps for those reasons I began to change. Or maybe it was that the advancing age of my children into their adolescent and teenage years strained against my rigid rule. Or it could even be some sort of innate need within me—as with all people—to grow and not sit stupidly in a forty-year-old body acting out of a twenty-year-old's value system.

I really don't know the reasons for these changes; all I know is that I find myself today listening to different voices. Some of the voices are my children's, and they're louder than before. Sometimes they whine, sometimes they argue, but often they are communicating with me. My willingness to change has prompted within them a greater confidence in their judgments and the security of knowing they will be heard. In gaining that security, they've had to sacrifice the comfort of knowing exactly where their once-unbending mother stands and how she will react. They—like the rest of us—want it all. They want to have the freedom to express themselves and make more of their choices, but at the same time be able to turn to the comfort of an unchanging mother—much like a childhood teddy bear that can be resurrected from a storage box at their bidding.

Generally their protests about my unfairness are really a protest against change. They probably don't realize this. Nor do they understand the depth of the growth I've experienced. They list perhaps a dozen or so examples of how my changing has hurt or disappointed them, and those are just a few, and minor at that, ways in which they've seen me change. More numerous are the subtle ways in which I've evolved into a more caring, a more aware person. Somehow, I sense a movement toward being more complete. Maybe this is what it means to mature. It might frighten my children if I were to tell them that the woman they see before them is not the woman who taught them their alphabet and how to eat from a plate. I wish I could explain to them how much they've had to do with the joy I find in this growth, but I won't because that's not what they want to hear. They want—maybe even need—a mother who's a consistent presence in their lives. They seem to push me into being like a snapshot they can take from their wallet or purse and say, "This is my mother." I don't tell them I've changed. And I certainly don't tell them that I'm not done yet.

The Simplicity
Of Now

*Children enjoy the present because
they have neither a past nor a future.*
—Jean de La Bruyere

When we say *generation gap* maybe what we mean is *time warp.* Living in a house with children is like being thrust into a science fiction plot in which people know the others are there but can't see or hear them. We live at the same address but in different times. My children live in this moment, right now, the present; I function quite often in what was or what might be.

Our language defines the time problem very nicely. My sentences begin with "Did you..." and "Are you going to..." Their tongues speak only present tense: "I'm going to the show." "I hear you." "You make me so mad." Even when they are recounting something in the past, they tell it as a current event: "Mr. Smith tells me my paper is late, and I go, 'Well, I handed it in with the others.' And he sends me down to the library to redo the assignment..." Communication? Impossible! What common ground is there for a mother whose time frame leaps from the heaviness of World War II to the fear of World War III as she tries to relate to children whose concepts of past and future are a whomping "Where did I put my retainer after breakfast?" to "What's for dinner?"

These are not ignorant, insensitive kids, but maybe that's just it—they're kids. They're young and still discovering the many large and small joys in living. They haven't yet gained what we parents call levelheadedness and realism; so instead of reliving the past and planning the future, they just live.

Interestingly, another group of people also lives happily in the present, and that is people my parents' age. Many people in the generation ahead of me seem to find that same kind of supreme joy in the simple details of the present. They, too, explore and rejoice in the everyday events of their lives. The past and future are important to them, but the happiest older people I know seem to put less value on them than I do.

I wonder about my role in all of this. Am I a fool surrounded by far wiser generations? Are my values misplaced in trying to amend, correct, and reflect on yesterday's events in order to plan, direct, and organize tomorrow's dreams? Am I sacrificing what should be the most productive and fulfilling portion of my life by never living in it?

These questions are confusing; what answers there are, are less than precise. Yes, I probably have been too preoccupied with what has been and what might be. And yes, I can make changes in the ways I use each moment. And I will try.

Yet, when I begin to think of the changes that can be made to help me live more fully and appreciatively in the present, the changes have to do with my children and with my older friends and relatives. And I begin to wonder again about my role. Is part of my concern with past and future a reflection of my relationship to the generations preceding and following me? Am I the bridge between what was and what will be? Once more, the abstract questions have only inexact answers.

But even these maybe-yes-maybe-no conclusions give me some comfort and direction. I *can* make more of an effort to live one day at a time. Lunch with a friend can be a joy and not an intrusion into a busy schedule. Even a short walk each day would force me to let time stand still and to clear my mind of frantic thoughts of yesterday and tomorrow. I can meditate. I can slow down. But I also can better understand the time warp between the generations.

All of us are right where we should be. The youngest ones live in the present because they sense no past or future. The oldest ones also live in the present, perhaps because they've earned that right. And those of us in the middle struggle to live in the present with them while reaching back with one hand and forward with the other—affirming the value of the past and the dreams of the future.

Breathing Room

But let there be spaces in your togetherness.

—Kahlil Gibran

All relationships need spaces, whether they be marriage, friendship, or parent-child. When I don't allow my spouse or my children some distance from me, I'm implying that either they are helpless or I am. Many times I've forced myself into their private moments because I was afraid they didn't need me, or they were making a mistake, or they were leaving me behind.

Often these people, and especially my children, have pushed me away and left me behind. Frequently they make the very mistakes I could have helped them avoid. *I* could have told them a car that costs $150 is going to be *verry* expensive. *I* would have told them no one can write a term paper in one evening, if they'd only asked. But they don't ask. In fact, they sometimes seem determined to do anything—bungle their way through, pay more money, even fail—anything rather than ask me. At those times, I try to listen to my mother's advice. She says, "They're good kids, and they have to learn some things their own way. Give them some space." Not so strangely, it's difficult for me to listen.

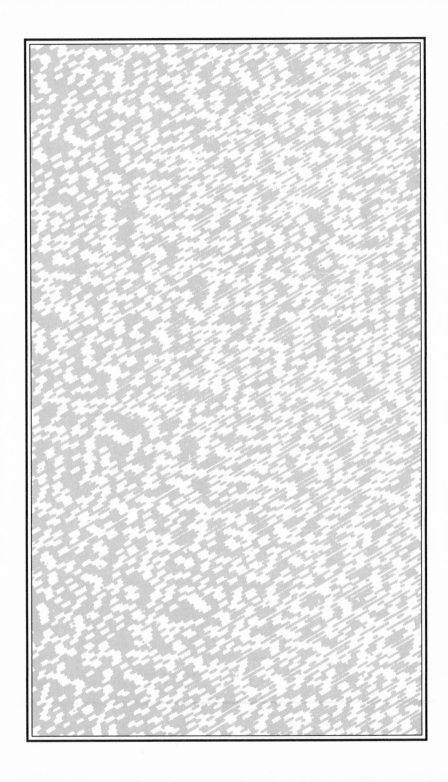

For Sale: 1 Camper

Nothing is intrinsically valuable; the value of everything is attributed to it, assigned to it from outside the thing itself, by people.

—*John Barth*

This couple would buy the camper; it was obvious from the moment they looked at it in our side yard. What salespeople call "buying signs" were clearly written across their faces and underlined in their words. Before they'd even asked the price, they were hatching plans for replacing the cushions, getting a spare tire, and talking to the bank about a loan. I told her I had washed the curtains and hadn't put them up yet. "Oh, don't," she said, "I'd just take them down again because I have some fabric at home that I'll use to make some new ones. But don't throw them away; I can use them as a pattern." After a full inspection of water tanks, the gas refrigerator, stove, oven, bathroom (no tub or shower)—after the table had been turned into a bed, the couch had unfolded into another bed, and the top board at the far end had been thumped down into yet a third (sleeps six uncomfortably)—after all this, plus the tarred roof being carefully inspected for leaks (none), then they asked what our price was. If they showed any reaction to our stated price, it was unexpected pleasure. They were going to buy it, I was sure. I hoped I was wrong.

I wasn't. "We'll take it," he said, without even conferring with his wife. Undoubtedly, he was as astute in measuring buying signs as I was.

"Well..." my husband said. I knew he wanted me to fill in the sentence.

"That's done," I obliged. My voice sounded hollow. Without another word to each other, we went back into the camper to look at it once again. I was seeing it again for the first time. The people who would soon own it had said so many of the same things we had when we'd fallen in love with it. It was cute, like a playhouse on wheels. Everything in miniature and so compactly organized. I remembered our first camping trip—the excitement and freedom of moving our little home from place to place—the magic of stopping wherever we wished and, presto, having lunch around the table and then taking off again.

The camper had been part of our lives for...how long? We weren't quite sure, but longer than Fritz, our dog who had lived with us for as long as our younger son could remember. Nine years, maybe, but more like ten or eleven. Longer than we'd owned any house, certainly.

I opened the cupboard above the stove and tiny sink and removed the greeting cards. They represented many years of Mother's and Father's Days and wedding anniversaries. Many were store-bought; more were tablet paper greetings, hastily scribbled by small children who had forgotten an occasion until zero hour. "Hapy mother day" proclaimed one in purple crayon. "Love Todd" was the closing on another, which had always struck me more as an instruction on parenting than as a signature. I took the cards and left dreading the next few hours.

We'd told the children we were thinking about selling the camper only a few days earlier but hadn't even advertised it yet. We had wanted to give them a little time to prepare for the loss. Then quite by chance, our friends had said they were looking for a camper. We're going to sell ours, we'd told them. Could we take a look at it? Certainly, it's on the north side of our house. And then...the camper was sold.

And now what? How would our children react to the suddenness of this? I could picture their faces—disbelief, possibly anger, and perhaps even tears. It was unfair to do this all so quickly. So much of their lives had centered around this blue-shelled entity. To them, it represented fun, excitement, some of our happiest family times—a trip to Wyoming to see Grandpa, two weeks in Estes Park and Denver, the Black Hills, fishing, swimming, and dozens of state parks. How many times had we built a bonfire at our campsite, roasted hot dogs, made "smores," and tempted curious chipmunks to our hands with peanuts? How many times had we played card games, board games, or just colored or read while we waited out sudden cold spells or rainstorms within the camper?

I feared telling them the news and prepared a litany of logical reasons for selling the camper. They knew the reasons already, but in expectation of their reactions I decided to tell them again. Selling it *was* reasonable. After all, we hadn't taken a trip or gone camping in more than two years. Too many family members with too busy schedules to make a family trip. Children who had grown up and whose bodies were now too large to comfortably fit into the same beds that once engulfed them. What use the camper now had was slight—occasional use as a spare summer bedroom and a clubhouse of sorts for the children and their friends.

We told them, and their response was much better than I'd expected—disappointment, yes, and a few moans—but their weak protests told me they'd already begun to accept it. Everything would be all right. They even did most of the packing up of personal belongings still in the camper. They carried in box load after box load of assorted treasures and enjoyed reminiscing over the contents.

Coloring books with signed and dated artwork received the most attention: "Look at this one. I colored it when I was five, and I thought it was so good."

"Well, it *is* good," I protested.

"Look at this thing I drew. Good thing I wrote 'Fritz' under it or you wouldn't know what it was."

I didn't look through the boxes; instead, the children were directed to carry them all to the basement where I'd go through them "sometime." The entire process took a surprisingly short time, and the camper stood ready for the new owners when they arrived to take possession.

My husband went out to take care of last-minute details, and I busied myself inside the house, relieved that the children had taken this all so well. Actually, I was more surprised than relieved. We'd given up so much in this sale.

My husband entered the house. The camper was gone. I looked at him and realized that the torn, lost, almost mournful expression on his face was a mirror of mine. A shared experience beyond words brought us together, and we held each other amid deep sighs and soft moans. We were alone; our children were nowhere near, almost as though they knew we would not handle this very well.

Surprise

*Why did the children put beans in
their ears when the one thing we told
the children never to do was put
beans in their ears?*
—Carl Sandburg

Why am I surprised to discover yet another frightening or destructive thing my child has done? Why did I think that the boy who, at age twelve, wore new tennis shoes into the swamp to catch frogs would not, when he was fourteen, check to see if the vacuum would suck up the dog's water? Why was I shocked when my younger son sniped at ants on the side of our stucco house with yellow spray paint, when only weeks earlier he had jumped into and broken 23 bags of leaves? Why do they surprise me?

My expectations must be wrong. I've had the idea that, as my children go about their day, they really consider how their parents will respond if they do such-and-such, but obviously they give little or no thought to us or our anger or a possible punishment. Instead of that adult fear of making a mistake, that fear of disappointing, they have an insatiable curiosity, a wonderment about "What would happen if?. . ." My children don't intend to hurt or challenge me. In fact, they're surprised that I'm surprised.

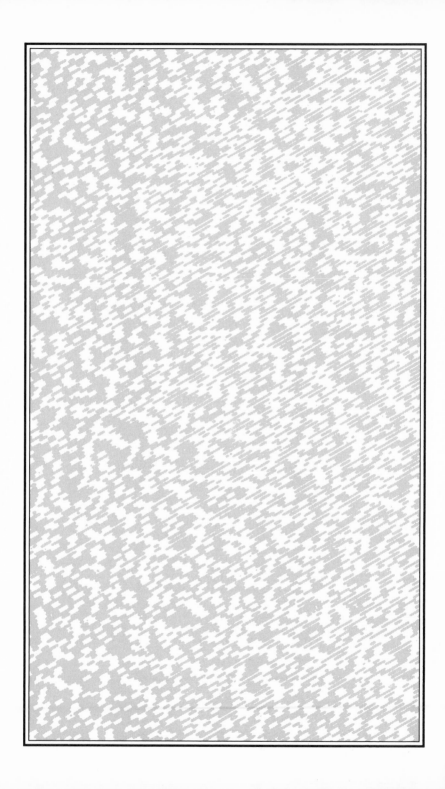

Protecting My Young

Any device whatever by which one frees himself from the fear of others is a natural good.

—*Epicurus*

She was nine years old and in third grade when we moved that October. There'd barely been time for her to adjust to a new teacher in one school, when whiz! bang! we plopped her into another school. The immediate change in her was noticeable; she was tired, irritable, and unable to sleep well. We dismissed it as a time of adjustment—new school, new friends, new teachers—until one night, several weeks after our move, she called for me once again from her bedroom.

"Mom, I still can't sleep," she explained as I sat on the edge of her bed. This was at least the fourth time she'd called me in to tell me that, and I was beginning to run low on patience.

"Well, you can sleep if you just lie here quietly and think sweet thoughts," I told her in a businesslike manner. Even to me the words sounded inane, but what else could I say? Or even do? We'd exhausted my small store of motherly remedies the second or third night of her sleeplessness. Cuddles, talks, warm and cold milk, drinks of water—nothing had helped.

"No, I know I can't," she whined, and she sat up in bed. I knew I should hold her, that she expected it, and probably that she needed it. Instead, I resorted to what I used when all else failed—anger. It wasn't a pretense; I was angry and frustrated. This pattern had become a nightly occurrence most evenings. I even wondered if these productions were just an elaborate manipulation on her part.

"Now, that's enough of this. Lie down and close your

77

eyes. You're tired. Just look how late it is, and both your brothers have been asleep for hours. You can sleep, if you decide you want to." I gently, but firmly, leaned her backward onto her pillow and stood up. My walk was confident, a real mother-in-charge stride, as I walked into the hallway and pulled the door shut. Once there, though, hopelessness ripped through that thin business-like exterior, and I felt myself slump in despair. I turned back to the door and bent forward with head turned to listen. *She was crying.*

There was no use going back in since I could do nothing for her; she couldn't explain the sleeplessness, and there was also a good chance I'd be encouraging an unhealthy pattern. But I went back in and held my daughter. Whatever put the question in my mind, I'm not sure, but as she leaned against my chest I asked her, "What do you think about when you lie in bed at night and can't sleep?"

"I worry about school."

"Are you worried about assignments?"

"No."

"Well, what then?" And she told me—she was scared of being yelled at by a certain teacher. We talked until I had the story straight. This teacher, according to my daughter, was very nice to her, but she yelled—and yelled often.

"Did she yell at you today?"

"No, she's never yelled at me, but she yelled at the boy next to me."

"Well, honey, you said she yells at students when they misbehave or deliberately try to bug her. Now, you've never been a problem to teachers, so don't you see—she's not going to yell at you."

"But—." Her face wrinkled up as she tried to stop the tears already welling up in her eyes. "But I can't stop the worry."

I was moved by such tender feelings for her and for

the need to protect her. Enough of this, I decided. A nine year old should not have to lie awake with fears like this. I gave her a hug, kissed her, and leaned her backward onto her pillow. "You just go to sleep," I told her, "and let your mother worry about this."

"Will you?" she said excitedly.

"Will I what?"

"Will you worry for me?"

"Well sure." I hesitated, knowing she'd misunderstood my meaning. But she sounded so reassured by the idea, that I said, "Sure, I'm going to be up for a while anyway. I'll worry for you."

After I agreed to do her worrying for her, my little girl squirmed over onto her side and promptly went to sleep. Our nighttime pattern from then on was the same as always, except when I approached the door to leave, she would call out, "Worry for me." And I'd reply, "I will. I'll worry." Occasionally she'd say, "Oh, no, that's okay. You don't have to. Tomorrow is Saturday." Every night for more than six months I worried for her (except Friday, Saturday, and holiday evenings).

I never fully understood the thought process in her ability to put her fears into my care and trust me to carry them. At her age then, she certainly must have known that my worrying would do no good, no matter what the problem. But, somehow, someway, she found comfort in letting me worry for her even though I had no control over the situation.

That was eight years ago. My daughter's fears have disappeared. In fact, if anything, she's fearless. Oh, she swings up and down in the customary teenage fashion, but she's confident and enthusiastic as she strides into adulthood. And our conversations are predictably different.

"Lock the doors when you're baby-sitting," I caution her. She tells me not to worry.

"Check to be sure you have enough gas in the car,"

I call out to her back as it disappears out the door. A chipper "Don't worry" is tossed over her shoulder.

"Call home if you'll be late," I tell her.

"I will. So don't worry."

"Shouldn't you be studying for your test?"

"Don't worry."

"Do you have enough money for your trip?"

"Don't worry, Mom," she stresses.

Don't worry. Don't worry. Increasingly, she draws the line between us, the line that all adults need to define their independence. I understand it, I respect it, and I even welcome it as evidence of her readiness to move on. Somewhere between her confidence that nothing can go wrong and my fears that something might is the reality of what her life will hold, and her gentle push to move me aside says she is ready. She's adapted more quickly to this change than I have. I feel a twinge of regret when I realize how little help I am to her now. A mother's kiss can no longer make everything better. She finds no comfort or peace in my worrying for her. For a while, though, as I adjust to our new relationship, I'll continue to worry, not because I have any delusions that it comforts her, but because it comforts me.

Popularity And
Peer Pressure

A President cannot always be popular.
—Harry S. Truman

It seems so obvious. It's only natural that leaders of any sort—presidents, popes, or kings—cannot always be popular, yet so often we think parents can be. Or we try to be friends to our children. But it never works for me. Every time I feel that warmth of bonding with my children in friendship, I immediately feel the chill of that awesome power—peer pressure. Friendship, at my children's ages—whatever age each is at the time—means loyalty to person over principle, to group over individual. Friendship, too often to them, involves people-pleasing, and the hard fact is, parents are not in the people-pleasing business.

So my children and I aren't friends very often. Every so often I slip into that role, and it's comfortable for a time because they expect much less from me. But accepting a group mentality or setting myself aside is too great a price for that comfort, and I always betray our momentary friendships by using what they call "parent talk." I'm rarely popular.

One Day
At A Time

Sweet childish days, that were as long
As twenty days are now.
—*Wordsworth*

I awoke early in the morning, filled with enthusiastic plans for the day. Today brimmed with dreams, goals, and promises of growth.

I toddled down to breakfast at seven and left for school just before eight, carrying a brand-new box of crayons and a handkerchief with lunch money tied in one corner. School friendships were formed immediately, and several of us bonded in a special closeness as we played tag, read to each other, double-dated, and participated in drama and sports. By the time we graduated at ten-thirty, we cried at having to leave each other. In the next hour, I fell in love, took my first cigarette, drank beer for the first time, fell out of love, and graduated from college at eleven-thirty. I confidently sauntered from the auditorium armed with a minimal grade-point average. There was an extreme teacher shortage, and by noon I was tenured.

For nearly a half-hour I wandered aimlessly, but then happened upon a likely young man. After a brief courtship, we were married in a beautiful twelve-thirty service and set out upon the world with that wonderful assuredness of young people in love. The direction of our lives was clear. Our goals were set. We had no money, but that mattered not at all because all the time in the world stretched endlessly before us.

We held each other tenderly for a few moments, then rushed out to buy our first home. The closing was at a quarter to one, and our daughter—our first child—was born fifteen minutes later. I wanted to hold her forever and give her everything—all my time, all my love, total security and safety. The same impulses swept over me at one-fifteen and two o'clock when our sons were born. Fortunately, I had plenty of time to offer them, so I laid them down for just a few minutes to catch my breath. Whether I dozed off or what, I'm not sure. All I know is I woke up, and they were no longer small.

We spent an hour in the mid-afternoon shopping for clothes for their first days of school, which was very hectic because we also moved four times, had dozens of scout meetings, took a couple trips, and I was stymied for a few minutes with the thought that I was being buried alive. My midday crisis would no doubt have lasted longer, but for the need to drive my daughter to the orthodontist and fill out college registration forms.

It's now past six o'clock. My two older children are concerned with their future plans. They're asking questions: "What should I do?" "What am I going to do with my life?" I set dinner on the table and smile benignly at them.

"Oh, don't worry yet," I tell them. "You have your whole life before you." I clear the table and walk to the front door to watch my husband put their suitcases in the car. By seven, our youngest child will also be packed up. My husband and I will sit on the sofa and lean back and tell each other how our day has gone with the luxury of the entire evening before us.

Highways And My Way

Yelling at children to make them behave is like trying to drive a car with the horn.

Anonymous

Many times I've driven hurriedly through traffic only to be delayed by another driver's poor judgment or poor luck. It's frustrating, knowing I *have* to get to an appointment, then having to wait while some fool negotiates an illegal left turn or restarts his car. Sometimes I let my horn express my feelings: *"Hoooonnnk!* Get out of my way. I and my appointment are important. You're not, and you're in my way. *Hooooonnnnk!"*

I feel much the same when I yell at my children. I'm busy. I'm tired. There's so much to do in such little time. So I "honk" at them: "I said NO you can't go to the show." "I'm sick of looking at your room." "Well, at least get out of my way so I can get something done." Honking on the freeway doesn't move traffic; it only reveals my self-importance and coldness. Unfortunately, that's exactly what it does at home too. My yelling doesn't help my children; it only tells them that my concerns are more important than theirs. And that's not the message in my heart and not the message I want to give them.

The Conspiracy

The joys of parents are secret, and so are their griefs and fears; they cannot utter the one, nor they will not utter the other.

—*Francis Bacon*

Children have a gift for honest communication that we parents seem to lose somewhere between the moment we gaze upon our first child and the instant in which we describe our feelings about that moment. "She (or he) is beautiful," we sigh over the curled-up bundle. That's our first dishonesty, and it establishes a lifelong pattern from which most of us never escape.

Perhaps I'm overstepping here by saying "us" and "we," rather than "me" and "I." Devoted parents may rise up in protest screaming, "How dare you say that I lied when I said my baby was beautiful!" But I'm going to stick to my guns and use the plural pronouns. Now really, didn't we have at least a hazy idea of what our first baby would look like? Didn't we imagine that baby as rosy-cheeked, plump, and topped with a tousle of hair? Wasn't our vision more similar to a three-month-old child than a newborn—a Gerber baby or those older infants passed off as newborns in movies and TV? And, of course, what we got was a newborn—a squirming, gulping mass of protoplasm with crossed eyes, scaling skin, and either no hair or an enormous puff of dandelion fuzz. Wasn't there a moment in which we were taken aback in disbelief? Just a split second of reconciling what we had expected with what we got? This has nothing to do with love; we were overwhelmed with love for our children. This has only to do with that moment of proclaiming their physical beauty when, in fact, they were not exactly what we had expected. And that's only the beginning.

Children are notorious for never being, acting, or looking like what their parents expect. The unexpected can range from wondrous acts of kindness to the most shocking behavior. For two reasons, it seems to me, we parents end up never saying quite what we're thinking or feeling about our children. The first has already been discussed: they are always surprising us—for good and bad. This means we rarely dare put ourselves out on a limb by declaring their saintliness or devilishness because there's a good chance they will, with their very next action, make liars out of us. Say a child hates beets, turn around, and there that child will be delightedly spooning the vegetable in over a dripping red chin. "Oh, Johnny always calls if he's going to be late," we proclaim, and we can plan on sitting up until very late awaiting his arrival.

The other and more difficult reason we hesitate to discuss our parenting concerns has to do with our sense of appropriateness. There is a natural restraint within, not just parents, but families. We feel uncomfortable discussing the love, joy, intimacy, and happiness within our families because they're too personal or too difficult to explain, or because we fear the appearance of bragging. For other reasons, we rarely discuss the lows of family life. There are times when it is inappropriate to reveal the personal elements of our lives with our loved ones. Too often, however, we misname our motives for not talking with others about family problems. We might call it family pride or loyalty, but in many cases it is really guilt, or shame, or a fear of being different from other families. Then it isn't just loyalty or pride; it is secretiveness.

When I was a new mother, I thought I understood the need for healthy openness. I thought I was honest with myself and others. Eventually, I saw that what I was passing off as openness was really a smoke screen of words. I talked about feelings and plans and hundreds of day-to-day details. The more I talked, the more I isolated my feelings about my parenting. Without realizing I was doing it, I had fallen into a comfortable pattern of worry and secretiveness. All the time I had believed I was developing new family traditions and patterns, I had actually been living within the same framework in which I had been raised.

My childhood family had worked into behaviors that are common to most people who have lived with a chemically dependent person. "Peace At Any Price" should have been cross-stitched on a sampler and hung on our kitchen wall. As it turned out, we had little peace and paid a great price. We tiptoed around issues, avoided arguments, and worked on appearing to be a perfect family. The role of heavy or villain was thrust upon my father, and at times he played it to perfection. The term *alcoholic* didn't mean disease to us or to the community in which we lived; it meant low-life or inferior or irresponsible. Since all of those terms were unacceptable to us, we never discussed or even considered calling my father an alcoholic. Instead, we acted as though he were choosing to hurt and betray us. When he wasn't around we talked about his disgusting behavior and plotted and planned as to how to get him to decide to stop. Everything focused on him, and most of the family pains were attributed to his choosing to drink. Despite all of our discussions within the family, we never talked of Dad's drinking to anyone outside. As far as I can remember, no one ever said, "We must not tell anyone else." It was just understood that the secret must be kept. I lived with a sense of guilt that it was my fault. I lived in fear that others would discover my guilt.

My gradual understanding of how these feelings and patterns had followed me into adulthood led to a corresponding awareness of them in my marriage and parenting. There, too, was a secretiveness and an overinflated idea of how much power and control I had over my husband and children, and this was followed closely by a sense of failure and guilt when any of them did not act as I thought they should. I was shocked by the similarities between the two families in which I'd lived or, more accurately, by how I continued to conduct my life by rules and patterns that I'd learned so long ago. I was still trying to manipulate my happiness out of the conduct of others. My sense of achievement depended on family members' successes. It had been more than twenty years since I'd left my family home, and I was still focusing on anything or anyone except myself.

Words and ideas come more easily than actions, especially when the actions are reinforced with decades of repetition. I didn't suddenly manage to detach my sense of self from my loved ones' identities. In fact, I still struggle with it. I probably always will. But there is a strengthened resolve to lay the responsibility for my happiness, success, and growth on the only person over which I have any real control—myself. I no longer am obsessed with shielding my family or myself from the fact of life that we each are separate. The love and care I give to my children are healthier when they're not restricted by the need to have those children make me proud and to fill out a life that has no form without them.

Increasingly, as I move out of my secrecy, I find that many other parents, for whatever reason, are reluctant to discuss their parenting doubts and fears. At one time I would have thought that perhaps others didn't have any of those negative aspects in their lives, that I was the only parent in the world who knew guilt. But no longer. It seems, instead, that we may be wrapping ourselves in a cocoon with iron strands of guilt, fear, and secrecy. I still hesitate to open myself to public scrutiny—old patterns die hard—but I'm more comfortable now with open communication. If we watch and listen to very small children, before they've been indoctrinated into our conspiracy of family silence, we can see how healthy their sense of identity is. Admittedly, sometimes they blurt out family intimacies or embarrass their families with inappropriate comments about the size, color, or shape of other people; but they are open and very clear about who they are, and they carry no guilt for the actions of others.

If our expectations of our children include only successes, good decisions, good looks, academic or athletic prowess—in a word: perfection—then we do our children a serious injustice. If we fear their failures and poor decisions as being a negative reflection on us, then we silently lock ourselves out of our own lives.

The world is filled with millions of parents who are convinced that they were given "perfect" babies and who are now filled with anguish over how they have failed them. If only we could talk to each other! What would we say?

"I'm afraid that my daughter's asthma is my fault because I smoked when I was pregnant."

"I think my son is using drugs."

"I'm sad because my children's friends are more important to them than I am."

"My son is doing poor work in school, and I don't think I help or encourage him enough."

"My children never have their friends over anymore."

"I think my teenager is sexually active, and I'm afraid to ask if it's true."

"I wonder if I should have had children."

"It seems like all my spouse and I do anymore is argue about the kids."

"I feel so alone."

There are so many times when we need a hug, a pat on the back, and a "There, there." We need to know that we're doing the best we can and that our best will have to be enough. We need to know that comfort is there for the asking, if we're willing to sacrifice our secrecy. We don't have to live with "Peace At Any Price" if the price is too high, nor do we have to harbor the guilt of having failed our children in some way or another. We all have regrets and weaknesses, but they become less menacing when we shed our cocoons. We can decide to do whatever is necessary—be more open with ourselves, share our concerns with a friend, join a parenting group, or find professional help if we're more comfortable with that. Uncovered, our unique secrets and concerns often look much smaller and less serious. They also look surprisingly like those of a million other parents.

The Burden
Of Detail

*To a worm in a horseradish, the
whole world is a horseradish.*
—Yiddish Proverb

"Ask him for the time, and he'll tell you how
to build the watch." The very first time I
heard that saying, I immediately thought of
several long-winded friends and acquaintances who
could be aptly described that way. A simple question
to them is met with a barrage of detail: no direct answer,
but a litany of description, explanation, and second
thoughts. I thought of a friend who adores long, drawn-
out phone conversations. Of a previous employer whose
every decision was liberally laced with subdecisions to
fit unexpected contingencies. I thought of a college
professor's meandering lectures. I thought of many other
people, but I didn't think of me.

Then I thought of me. How many times had one or
the other of my children come to me with a simple request only to be told to "wait a minute and listen to this."
The "this" being a letter to the editor, a poem, or a
powerful passage in one of the books I'm reading.

It was shocking to picture myself in the company of
those other people, especially since I think of them as
dull. Could it be my children think of me as dull?
Impossible! I'm interesting, exciting, and lead a busy life.
I'm working at researching. For fun, I proofread. Two
of my most appreciated birthday gifts were an un-
abridged dictionary and *The Chicago Manual of Style*.

My horseradish is words. I thrive on seeking correct,
even preferred, spellings. I anguish over my love of the
dash. My desk is littered with magazines, books, and
newspapers. I write down colorful phrases and words

93

that are new to me. Could my children think this dull? Sadly, I admit, of course they do. Just as dull as the horse-radishes in which my friend, a boss, and the college professor live. They, like me, expect others to share their intense interests and would probably be just as shocked to learn that they are dull.

I'm more interesting to my children and more effective as a parent if I talk less commas and classics and more fashion and funk. That's not dishonest; it's meeting them in their reality. I get their attention when I show I'm knowledgeable about the height of hems and the name of a running back. My life is more than books and words, so the better I'm able to show them the full range of my awareness, the clearer they see me.

The Reality
Of Children

*Fairyland is nothing but the sunny
country of common sense.*
—*G. K. Chesterton*

Children provide parents with a second chance to dream and wonder. They, in all innocence and wide-eyed belief, pull us out of our ho-hum reality into the world as they see it. And often what they reveal to us is more real and alive than what we offer them. Was my opinion of dandelions more valid than that of my older son who, from the time he was allowed to toddle outdoors, spent most of the springtime gathering huge bouquets of the weed? He forever changed me. I see their color now and understand the joy he had in their discovery. Each spring gives me the chance anew to remember a little yellow-nosed boy eagerly offering me his treasure: "These are for you, Mom."

What parent hasn't been given similar opportunities to once again marvel at the moon's ability to follow the family car returning home late at night. "Look at the moon. It's following us!" At those times, we don't explain it away; instead we join them in their amazement because, in our adult straightforward way, we had forgotten to really look at the moon. We had grown up and lost our ability to see the magic around us, but our children excitedly tug at our sleeves, pointing and wanting to share. They help us see and remember.

My own children returned that magic to me many years ago. We were returning home along a gravel road. The summer evening had turned cool, and wisps of fog were creeping across the road. In the back seat, the children were intently peering out the window. Every once in a while, I'd hear one say, "There's one!" And they'd

95

hush each other as though they didn't want me to hear.

"Do you see the lightning bugs?" I asked.

There was no immediate reply, but finally my daughter said, "No, we're watching for the fairies."

Suddenly, I understood their interest. I had told them we would take the Ferry Road home. My first thought was to explain the difference between "ferry" and "fairy," but instead I silently listened to them as they spotted the little beings in the cattails and grasses along the road. I remembered my own interest in fairies as a child and how I, too, had seen them among my grandmother's hollyhocks. I was able to recapture the sense of contentment I had found in believing that there were living creatures who were like me but—more important— were so much smaller than I was. My children's misunderstanding of the word "ferry" reminded me of the Rainbow Bridge near my hometown. As a little girl, I hadn't realized the name was derived from the arches on each side of the structure and had believed, instead, that either the bridge took on the colors of the rainbow after a storm or that all rainbows originated on the bridge. Now the bridge has a traditional square-sided shape; it was rebuilt after the flooding creek destroyed it one year, but it continues to be called the Rainbow Bridge.

It was pleasant to recall these fantasies of my youth, and I decided not to give my children an adult, common sense explanation about there once having been a ferry across the river where this road ends. And what sense would it make to a child, anyway, to tell them that adults feel it is reasonable to call this the Ferry Road, even though no ferry has been near it for 30 years or more? Someday, I decided, I'll tell them about this. And about a square rainbow. And about my grandmother laughing and calling my vigil in her hollyhocks a waste of time. I slowed down the car because the fog had suddenly become worse—and my children needed a better chance to see the fairies.

The Name Of
The Thing

*The beginning of wisdom is to call
things by their right names.*
—*Chinese Proverb*

My memory tells me they descended upon us unannounced, these strangers somehow known by my parents. A nine year old's excitement over the unexpected was transformed into an entirely different and foreign emotion, however, by the end of the day. My family didn't have a word for the man's behavior at dinner that evening. It probably had a name even then, but we didn't know it. And my fear, too, went unnamed because adults were not to be feared in the early 1950s. Instead, I felt sick—a more acceptable reaction.

The afternoon had been a pleasant break from the usual farm routine. The adults visited in the house while my younger brother and I played with the little boy and girl outside. When dinner, "supper" for us, was called out by my mother, we scampered in with the excitement of this new adventure still upon us. The man, his wife, son, and daughter sat immediately at one end of our large kitchen table, and my mother, father, brother, and I filled the remaining spaces. The woman served herself from the offered dishes and then fixed a small plate for the two-year-old boy, while the father helped himself and the girl, who was four. As each dish came around, he asked her gently if she wanted some. Seeming not to hear her negative answers, he placed a portion of everything on her plate, and it later seemed to me that he gave her larger helpings of the food she refused. After she had eaten the foods she liked, her father told her to finish eating. She looked straight ahead and

97

moved her head in a no. Within fifteen minutes we witnessed their escalating confrontation—he moving from threats to screaming rage and she quietly refusing. Finally, he moved his arm behind her, grabbed the top of her hair, and sharply yanked her head backward. Her mouth flew open in a yowl. He shoved a large spoonful of food in and, with his free hand, forced her chin up to close her mouth. She struggled as though drowning.

I instinctively looked toward my mother, expecting to see her rise up in fury with much the same look on her face as those times I was caught taunting my brother. But her face was turned downward due to a sudden and inexplicable interest in our years-old dinnerware. I looked around the table; couldn't anyone else hear those muffled croak-like cries? My father was intently appraising the value of a stainless steel spoon, his mouth slightly askew as he examined the spoon's front, back, and front again. The mother, equally unhearing, was dabbing her napkin—needlessly and repeatedly—around her son's small face.

The only sounds were from the girl and from her brother as he quietly protested the napkin's lengthy use. Time and reality seemed to be twisted out of shape. Something here was wrong. I knew it, and I knew that my parents did too. But then, why didn't they do something? My fear suddenly deepened with a terrible thought: were my parents also afraid?

A loud gulp. She had swallowed! I looked up in relief, only to see the man remove his hand from her chin and thrust another spoonful into the little mouth as it snapped open. I turned to my brother beside me and grimaced to indicate we shouldn't stare, and we looked downward. In this manner the girl finished her meal. Every evening was the same; they stayed for eight days.

Society's attitude toward children has changed dramatically since then, but some things—like fear—haven't. I know the correct name for what I witnessed at our dinner table long ago, and the very fact that it *was* far in the past makes it even easier for me to smugly give it its proper name. And that it involved strangers—people my parents knew only remotely, people I never saw again—gives even greater emotional distance and safety when I apply a label to a man who force-fed a four year old.

My children strip me of that safety and distance in the here and now. What they need from me is what I needed from my parents—a sense of order, a sense of rightness, and the reassurance that their perceptions are correct. Each has come to me, bewildered and concerned, and asked my opinion of a family we know. The man and woman are close friends of ours, but the families see each other only infrequently because we live a ways apart. Yet, the aftermath of each meeting is the same: my children come to me and, without ever really saying it, ask me to put the word we all know to what we have witnessed. "Well," I waffle, "they are stricter than your dad and I are." I wonder if they recognize the fear in me.

Do my children feel betrayed? Is it dishonest not to tell them of my own similar reactions? Should I tell them I have called the toll-free number to talk to someone who understands this behavior? Would they understand my reluctance better if I told them about discussions with pastors, medical people, and a lawyer—all of whom urged caution. My concerns and those of my children don't center on specific, physical actions as much as a pervasive atmosphere in which two children are frequently belittled, ridiculed, and disciplined in ways I believe are inappropriate.

When I anguish about the severity I've seen, I better understand my mother and why she stared at an empty plate unable to help a tortured child. The fear is still there. The fear of being wrong or of making things worse. When faced with behavior so bizarre or so different from our own, we doubt ourselves and even the reliability of senses. Do I see this in proper perspective? Does this seem extreme only because I am too lax with my children? Those children are well-groomed, and it's obvious that even the smallest details of their lives are conscientiously attended to, which is often more than my children can say. Am I wrong about their treatment of their children? Possibly. Do I hesitate because I fear a counterattack on my own vulnerable parenting? Very possibly. Would my friends understand my loving concern if I talked to them? Definitely not.

How do I find my way out of this emotional struggle between loyalty, even love, for the parents and responsibility to the children, especially when there is some chance I'm wrong and tremendous odds that nothing could be done even if I'm not? I lie awake sometimes and see those children, and I know that the physical pain I experience must be heartache. The pull within me to name what I see is so very great. My children come to me with the same expectations I had so long ago: *Make it right: say the name of the thing.* And, God forgive me, I can't. I'm only able to give it a name when I tell about the family who came to visit. The man was the son of a family my mom and dad once knew... strangers really....

The Tablecloth

*A cloak is not made for a single
shower of rain.*

—*Italian Proverb*

My grandmother's hand-crocheted table-cloth lies carefully folded and protected by tissue, neatly tucked in the chest with my wedding dress and the newspapers from the dates of my children's births. It is unused. It is untouched, except for the periodic rearranging of the chest's contents. With my young daughter at my side, I used to methodically remove everything and then, with equal care, straighten and return each item. There would always be a predictable dialogue between us. She would ask the origin and importance of the treasures, and I would patiently explain. Reverently kneeling before the chest, we acted out the rites I had learned as a child.

When I was small, during each fall and spring cleaning, my mother and I would clean the cedar chest. As she removed the items, I identified them and recited their histories.

"And this is the tablecloth that Grandma made, isn't it?" I'd ask, as she set aside the war coupons and baby books.

"Yes," my mother would say. "She worked for months to make it. And she did it with love." Mother would then spread the cloth so we could see the lovely intricacies of the stitches, and she would remark how beautiful it would be on our table at a special dinner like Thanksgiving or Christmas.

My mother never used that tablecloth. Neither have I. Whenever the thought strikes me that *now* would be the time to use that cloth, I opt instead for one less precious—an oilcloth, a drab print bought on sale, plastic placemats, or even paper things to be thrown away immediately.

My grandmother crocheted the tablecloth when she was in her sixties. Her children were grown, and, no doubt, she had more love hours at her disposal. A woman's sixties must be a reflective age, a time in which she can more objectively view the joys and disappointments, the accomplishments and failures of her life. I've noticed this in my own mother. She now speaks more of how children should be raised, of how they're gone before you know it, and of how parents must wisely use that short time. These words are like the tablecloth— the product of time and wisdom, the distillate of mistakes and the need to share.

The advice and the tablecloth—they are treasured and honored but unused. I spread them out from time to time. I admire them as offerings of love from two women I respect but who, I know, used everyday tablecloths all their lives.

My daughter will probably marry some day, and I will give the tablecloth to her. I will plead with her: "Use this. It is meant to be used. Don't make the mistake I did." I'll tell her, too, when she's a mother to use the all-too-little time wisely with her children. I know she'll hear me. I know she'll understand me. And I know she'll store them away, save them, and finally use them—but only when the time comes to hand them down to her children in our time-honored ritual.

The Bunk Bed

*When I was a child, I spake as a
child, I understood as a child, I
thought as a child; but when I became
a man, I put away childish things.*
— *1 Corinthians 13:11*

My son moans in protest as I snug the covers
under his chin. Even in sleep he defends
his increasing independence and with-
draws from this nighttime ritual of childhood. This evening I've come to tuck him in, despite his assurance that
it's no longer necessary, and realize I do this for myself.
I intended to honor his request that we say our good
nights downstairs, but after a while my unease became
too great. A vague feeling of unfinished business swept
over me, much like remembering an important job not
done. I've come to check "just one more time" and hope
he doesn't awaken and catch me in this betrayal. Slowly,
I lower my weight to the side of his bed.

We "de-bunked" the beds today. For five years this
bed has been a fantasy world for him, not just one bed
atop another. It has been a cave, a hidey-hole, a cloud.
A menagerie of stuffed animals and super heroes once
slept with him, played with him, and listened to his
secrets in this never-never land. Tonight the toys are
packed away, and he sleeps solemnly in a bed depend-
ably anchored to the floor.

The faint light from the hallway contorts the contents
of the room—my shadow is hardly visible against the
wall, while my son's form beneath the covers seems en-
larged, elongated in the half-light. He moves in a dream-
stir; the full length of the covers wraps closer to his body.
I'm amazed—like a friend or family member who hasn't
seen a child for a long time—to realize how grown up
he really has become. It's not the grayness of the room

that has confused reality; my own mind has done that. The boy I saw but minutes ago is gone. I kiss the round, fleshiest part of his cheek; it is soft, but barely.

The Father
Of My Children

Marriage—a book of which the first chapter is written in poetry and the remaining chapters in prose.
—Beverley Nichols

February is a strange time in which to celebrate Valentine's Day. February is unromantic, at least for us in the Midwest. Here, this month is the height of the snow, cold, and flu season; it means mud, slush, and dreary days. Why February? I would wonder. Why not June, already agreed upon as a month of romance and marriage?

We were married in June, my husband and I. The day was a warm, flower-scented day—just the kind of day I'd envisioned and planned for. Looking back, I feel foolish to admit I had no contingency plans for rain; I knew the day would be perfect, just as I knew the years ahead would be. How could I expect otherwise? We were in love, but not like other couples. We were so open; no secrets for us. We were kind. I felt as though we had been picked in some heavenly lottery to be given the perfect marriage. We had known each other for a year— and forever. In that year we had spent hundreds of hours together, or on the phone, or writing to each other. My husband-to-be had even written a love poem for me, and I had opened up my deepest emotions in letters to him.

Nearly seven years later, I spent Valentine's Day thinking a lot about my wedding day. That year, February 14 was a perfect backdrop for my dark mood. Outside the kitchen window, the trees were wet-black against a gray sky. Their branches were stiff and unbending in the wind. The recent snowfall was already dirtied in the February melt, and scattered patches of unpromising brown grass lay idle like puddles in the yard. Inside, the house felt cold. Even the sounds of the three children failed to brighten our home; the voices of the older two and the baby's coos seemed distant somehow. More accurately, I felt distant. Even when nursing my infant son, I felt as though I were watching—not participating in—this intimate mother-child experience.

I looked into the bathroom mirror and wasn't surprised by the woman who looked back at me. Her eyes were dull; her face had no color except the redness around her eyes and nose. Although I knew much of my appearance was due to the flu I'd had for three days, it seemed impossible that this sadness and despair would ever pass. I looked down at the robe I was still wearing so late in the morning and could visualize the body underneath: the skin less taut and permanently etched with stretch marks. I thought about getting dressed in case my husband came home for lunch, but didn't.

The sounds again of my children—calling, demanding— spurred no response in me. They seemed so far away. It was Valentine's Day, and I thought of my wedding day, when nothing was asked of me but to be beautiful and to move into a lifetime of flowers and love letters.

I'd like to report that my husband came home with flowers and suddenly I saw the meaning and beauty of my life. Twenty years ago I would have expected that to happen, but twenty years ago I expected to be taken care of. I lived with the greatest confidence that others could—and should—fix my pain, disappointment, or sadness. On the day I was married I expected the mantle of responsibility for me to be passed from my parents to my husband. That my husband had the same expectation probably explains our idyllic view of what our marriage would hold. We, too, had no contingency plans for rain.

The problems we have faced as a couple often occur when we have to let go of old patterns or expectations. The realities of living together have forced us to abandon hand-holding and empty declarations of love in favor of mutual support and acts of love. This isn't easy; it's painful to give up the known for the unknown. Usually, only hindsight allows us to see that we or our relationship has changed. Often, anger or arguments accompany our moves from Point A to Point B, and a great part of the pain is not knowing at the time that we're moving. Our adjustment is expressed sometimes as anger and sometimes as silence.

Many of the changes each of us makes are personal changes and have nothing to do with each other, yet we have to accommodate those changes within the framework of our marriage. And some of the things we've seen as change were not change at all, but a truthful revelation of what we always were. My husband is not a poet and has not written another poem in twenty years. In fact, he's asked me to destroy his one attempt at verse. And I'm not and never was as open as he and I once thought.

Each of us has a different relationship with our children, and some of our most heated arguments have to do with one of us wanting the other to change his or her approach to parenting. We've made progress in coming to terms with this problem and, for the most part, are able to not meddle in the other's parenting. We understand that he is more decisive and autocratic, that I am more likely to analyze and to be empathetic. He is more generous; I am afraid of spoiling our children. The children come to him when they want an immediate answer; they come to me when they have time to argue for a yes. They shop more with him and talk more with me.

My husband and I are at mid-life, whatever that means. We're in our forties, and we're experiencing some of the emotions we believed we were immune to. He is reevaluating his career and feeling the pressure of limited time obstructing his success. I am struggling to make up for the time I lost when others were taking care of me. We're both more independent.

We've been lucky. Through no foresight on our part, we each chose a mate who could accommodate change. Marriage has been mostly an enriching part of our lives. It has allowed itself to be bent and twisted into a form that we never expected twenty years ago, just as we have become completely different people from the two young- sters who made promises to each other on a warm summer day. We're lucky because, despite our changes, we willingly honor the commitment made by two know- it-all kids.

Each June we celebrate our anniversary, which is a fitting time to remember our decades-old dreams. But it is in February that I remember what my marriage really means, and I often think of that Valentine's Day thirteen years ago when I struggled with the reality of what my life had become. On that day my husband did come home for lunch and wished me a happy Valen- tine's Day. He gave me a card with a mushy verse, which he could have written but no longer would. I thanked him, blew my nose yet again, and let my aching body drop onto a chair. He rested on heels in a crouch beside my chair and put his arms around me. He told me I was beautiful.

Perhaps some marriages as long as ours still have poetry, music, and long walks along a beach. Ours doesn't, but it does have the stability of two people who love—and like—each other. It doesn't fear growth and change. We don't have that youthful fear of los- ing each other. Reality tempers our expectations: we know it might rain on our plans and we might not like or approve of everything the other does. We like Valentine's Day right where it is. Anyone can find beauty and love in the flowers and sunshine of June; we find them in the cold forbidding days of February.

Power Play

Patience is not a virtue if you sit back and wait for your problem to solve itself.

—*Robert H. Schuller*

Decisions are hard for me to make. Instead of jumping in and risking a mistake, I often postpone, procrastinate, and wait it out in hopes the problem will disappear. Even worse, I have the questionable talent of ignoring to the point of forgetting matters that require a decision. I try to pass this off as patience; but, in my most honest private moments, I know this to be a serious obstacle to both my maturity and parenting.

The children often can't get direct answers to their simplest questions: "Can I stay at Billy's?" "Will we be able to get me a new coat?" "Is it all right for me to baby-sit a week from Friday?" This indecision hinges on one primary issue—power. Perhaps I've unconsciously been using these postponing techniques to tie my children to me or to keep them aware of my power in their lives. If I have been doing this, I've been abusing the respect my children show me by asking. I need to make decisions more quickly for their sake and for mine. I don't want to needlessly or cruelly taunt them with my pretense of power. They need to be more free. I need to let them go.

The Value Of Money

There is no such thing as absolute value in this world. You can only estimate what a thing is worth to you.
—Charles Dudley Warner

In my most self-assured moments, I like to think of myself as a source of wisdom for my children, a revered presence in their lives to which they turn for advice and consolation. This puffed-up view of myself usually survives only a few minutes, however, into any conversation with them. While I might want to be a living, treasured book filled with worthwhile life experiences and observations for them to use, they dispatch me as quickly as yesterday's newspaper. Their message is clear: "Your life is not like ours. We are different. Listen to us." And when I do come down from my mountain and really listen, I often learn more from my children than they could learn from me. A recent lesson involved money.

They needed more money, they said. Their allowances were inadequate. "Everyone" had bigger allowances than they. I opened up my vast store of knowledge for them and explained how much more fortunate they are than their father and I were as children. We were not the beneficiaries of an allotted sum each week; instead, our parents doled out a quarter or a dollar here and there when they could afford to, which wasn't very often. And, I emphasized, we worked: their father at age twelve in a truck garden for 50 cents an hour, and I as a babysitter for the same amount. We got by on that small rate of pay by planning well and working hard. The value of money, I patiently explained to them, is not only a reflection of what you can buy but also of the work you do. Value yourself, I told them, and see your earnings as being a measure of your worth. I expected them to be impressed. They weren't.

If anything, they were angry. They picked apart my lecture, insisting that the comparison was unfair, that our childhoods are different and everything costs more now. I quickly countered their argument with a dramatic demonstration of how wrong they were. I took paper and pencil, sat down with them at the kitchen table, and showed my children how little they understood about money, values, inflation, and the importance of work. "Now here," I said in my first-grade teacher voice, "is the 50 cents I earned. And—let's use candy bars as a measurement—I could buy ten five-cent candy bars with my hour's work. And you make what? A dollar-fifty an hour baby-sitting?" I looked at my daughter and she nodded. "So what do candy bars cost?" They told me— forty-five cents. "So, with one hour's work, you are actually earning..."

I stopped. Something had to be wrong. It seemed impossible that I, in my less-than-prosperous youth, had enjoyed greater buying power than my children have now. Certainly, I couldn't have earned the equivalent of ten Hersheys an hour, while for the same labor my daughter receives three or four. I was stunned and looked up at my children. For the first time in weeks, I had their undivided attention. They leaned in toward the paper with bemused smiles.

"Maybe," I told them, "candy prices have outrun the inflation rate because of the cost of sugar. Let's use another comparison like movies or hamburgers." I scratched some more on the sheet before me. Although the figures weren't nearly as far out of line, they still glared the same message: My husband and I had, in our childhoods, greater buying power with our earnings than our children do with theirs. My husband earned two hamburgers for an hour's work; our children earn one at best. Two hours of baby-sitting gave me four movies and my daughter one.

Their allowances were raised that day by a percentage that I felt was outrageous yet justified by the figures on the paper. They were satisfied—both by the amount of their new allowances and by my willingness to reconsider and change my mind. They left the table, and I remained to ponder the conflicting emotions within me. First of all, I—like them—was pleased with my decision; I was proud that they had seen me approach their request so logically and then change my mind when faced with new information. But beyond the pride was a sense of future shock. Where have I been, I wondered. I'm like a person who awakes from a years-long coma to face an alien world and culture. The gradual changes, unnoticed by me through my adulthood, had built up to the time—just moments ago—when the world had seemed to transform in an instant. Candy bars don't cost five cents; a hamburger and malt are closer to four dollars than 50 cents.

I turned the paper over and continued to calculate the impact of inflation. A pattern showed itself clearly. The five- and ten-fold inflation was primarily in the items and services that children buy—candy, pop, movies, and snacks; while a pound of hamburger, a new car, houses, and salaries all were near the 300 percent rate. It was reassuring to see I wasn't totally out of sync with the world—minimum wage buys about the same amount of groceries today as it did when I was a child, and a $20,000 house bought then can be purchased for $60,000 now. I was going to call my children back and show them these figures to prove that their money's buying power was comparable to what mine had been. "Look here," I would tell them, "the value of money is in what it can buy. Nothing changes except the amounts; an hour's work today buys the same things it did when I was a child."

I didn't call them back, however, because I suddenly

realized that these figures had nothing to do with their reality—the price of candy bars, movies, records, makeup, and pop. For whatever reason—that kids have more money and the prices have soared to what the market will bear, or that production of these items has risen beyond the inflation rate—the only reality for them is what they can buy with their money. And their money doesn't buy as much as mine once did.

Suddenly
September

> *For man, autumn is a time of harvest,*
> *of gathering together. For nature, it is*
> *a time of sowing, of scattering abroad.*
> *—Edwin Way Teale*

It's probably just as well that I forget each year how quickly the fall descends upon us. If I remembered, I'd scamper around like the squirrels, trying to do all the things I'd planned last spring and, in doing so, would lose the most marvelous gift of autumn—forgiveness. As it is, I languish in the warmth of each endless summer and accept each bright, new day as an implied promise of another just like it to follow. Summer projects and goals are approached in a haphazard fashion—a little work on one here, a slight postponement on another there.

Suddenly, a particular damp chill—or is it an aroma?—surrounds me, and I'm surprised. The unmistakable colors of the trees confirm that fall is here to stay, and the standstill of winter is just a short distance off. The unfinished projects and plans chide my good intentions, and quickly I must decide which things can still be, which must be, finished before winter.

Then, a calmness sets in. The forgiveness of autumn gives me peace. It releases me from the have-tos and musts. Decisions are all at once easier. A family trip put off too long becomes an outing in the cities, combining some together time with school shopping. The trim on the house suddenly doesn't look too bad; it can wait another year. The garden, so long a reminder of my neglect, is turned over into a shining black promise for next spring. The graying of the western sky threatens colder, shorter days, and that reality pushes me into choosing and picking and prioritizing. I'm able to see which things I want to do before winter; the less necessary or unnecessary are let go of with no regret. They had never really mattered at all, and now the crisp autumn wind sweeps them from my mind. Quickly, I gather the last stalwart mums to adorn the dining room table. The cars are winterized. The lawn is given a light raking. The wind shifts sharply to the north; it bites at my arms as I run into the house with a load of wood. Soon, a fire makes strange shadows across the darkened living room. The sun has already set. I ease into the sofa and watch the flames, at peace with a summer well spent.

The Immigrant

*You cannot put the same shoe on
every foot.*
—*Publilius Syrus*

He likes to tell about the boat trip; you can see
it in his eyes as he talks. His mother decided
to leave Italy, so he, his mother, and two
sisters came across the ocean to this country when he
was twelve—more than 60 years ago. He clearly remem-
bers being frightened. He was frightened because his
family was leaving friends and all they knew behind.
He was frightened of the ship itself, which looked so
small against the vast ocean, but mostly he was frightened of the night. The rule was, they were told, that all
men twelve and older must sleep in the men's section
of the hold; smaller children and daughters could stay
with their mothers.

Naturally, he tells this story from his perspective, but
when I hear it, I sympathize—I identify—more with the
emotions of his mother than with his. Although we're
separated by two generations and vastly different
lifestyles, that woman and I are sisters, momentarily,
when I cringe inside with the anguish she must have
felt. All parents, at some time or another, are confronted
with the cruelty of rules that exist for the convenience
of authority rather than the concern for our children.
No exceptions, we're told. The implication is, don't fight
the system, rules exist for the good of all, don't put yourself above others.

We don't want to ask for special favors, nor do we want
to appear to think we're better than all the others who
follow the rules. In contrast to this is our need to do
what's best for our children and to not betray their trust

117

as they confidently wait for us to do the right thing.

But what is the right thing? Should I confront the science teacher who my child claims has deliberately lowered the final grade? Should I question the wisdom of not giving my child a Sunday School attendance certificate when his only absences were the times we were camping miles from civilization? Is it worth the risk of appearing self-important?

Usually, I've not been willing to take the risk and, instead, explain to the child the necessity for rules and how they protect us all. And the few times I've challenged the rules I can't say have given me great happiness or success. But there is a satisfaction in knowing I've done what I thought best. I have given my children the message that sometimes the individual is more important than the corporation, that no one rule can forsee all individual situations, and that a rule is meant to protect, not injure.

I'll probably never know how much, if any, effect my decisions will have on my children or if they'll even remember my choices. But I'm comforted by the Italian man who tells the story about himself as a twelve year old and the rule that said he was a man. I like his small laugh as he pulls me into the plot and tells me about the rule and about his fears. But mostly I love the look on his face when he talks about his mother's acceptance of the rule and her defiance of it. Even now—60 years later—he still exudes a little-boy pride in his mother who came to him in the men's sleeping quarters each evening, took the hand of her fatherless son, and brought him back with her to sleep within the security of his family.

Intellectualizing
The Obvious

*The moment the little boy is concerned
with which is a jay and which is a
sparrow, he can no longer see the
birds or hear them sing.*

—*Eric Berne*

"Oh, look! What's that?" We pushed our children's attention to kitties, puppies, babies, birds, rainbows, and thousands of other details of their world. Our parental egos were puffed up by what we chose to see as signs of their intelligence—early speech and large vocabularies. Perfect parents that we were, we urged our children into learning and performing.

It's difficult now to positively identify my new-parent motives. Some certainly were based on the best of intentions—language development, the child's self-confidence, and communication between us. Some motives, however, I think were less than noble. Although I can't remember exactly, I recall a vague sense of needing to prove something or to reassure myself. Perhaps I was displaying my children in much the same way that Scouts or science students arrange their best projects for public scrutiny and judgment. And there might have been a need to have my children shine and thereby dispel the nagging doubts I had about my ability to parent. But mostly I was prompted by my inner need to intellectualize.

The first time I heard the word *intellectualize* used in a less than complementary way was in a self-help group. We were discussing emotions, and various people had already talked about the difficulty they had dealing with specific emotions. Then I shared what I thought were my feelings. After I'd finished, another group member accused me of intellectualizing. At first, I was dumbfounded. Here I had opened up so willingly, and now I was being attacked. But after considerable discussion by many of the members, I began to understand what I had been doing at the meetings and, sadly, in most of my dealings with other people.

I had ignored many, maybe most, of the enriching aspects of life and had emphasized my mind. Somewhere along the line, I had found comfort in being thought intelligent. I had found peace and rewards in mental pursuits. And I had found something else—power—but it wasn't until the caring members of my group risked my anger by discussing this with me that I was able to see my passive intellectualizing for what it was. My need for power and control had always directed conversations into my comfort zone. Everything had an answer, if only it was thought about correctly. All problems could be solved. Any negative emotion could be eliminated if it were analyzed.

Patterns aren't broken easily. My first response to emergencies and crises is a belief that they can be corrected if I think about them enough. Whether mine or someone else's, a problem presented is too often held up immediately to examination. But I'm moving forward and have the advantage of second and third options now. Sometimes a problem has to take its own time to be resolved, and that requires patience. Sometimes the problem isn't even mine, and accepting that means detaching from the responsibility for solving it. Grief isn't a situation to be solved; it's a process, and the best I can do is turn to my God, my Higher Power, and ask to be carried along. A friend who comes to me for comfort usually isn't looking for words, but for human contact and comfort. Words add nothing to—in fact they detract from—the comfort my arms can give a grieving friend.

There are still times and situations that require level thinking and problem solving, and I work hard to recognize them. Now I continue to encourage my youngsters to build their communication skills, to expand their vocabularies, and to develop their minds, but I encourage them not to mistake mental skills for total living skills.

Maybe all children have an innate understanding of this truth. Even when they know the correct words for things, they often resort to the emotional level. At those times, an "Oh"—somewhere between a sigh and a prayer—is all they can say. I first heard this "Oh" when our daughter spotted a full moon. The glowing orange globe seemed so large and close that she reached out her hand as though to touch it—"Oh." More recently, on a family trip, we reached the crest of a small hill and were suddenly struck by the beauty of a Pennsylvania valley; "Oh," we all breathed. There are no more words to capture the thrill of being surprised by beauty.

Today my daughter left reluctantly for school, dreading the announcement of the cast for the school play. Last night she put it into words—her fear of not finding her name on the list, of being on the fringe of the camaraderie, of being embarrassed. Her audition wasn't good, she said, and the two teachers in charge are too fair to give any advantage to her experience in two earlier plays. Knowing this gives me time to prepare so, if she doesn't make it, I won't make the mistake of offering a minute interpretation of an emotional pain that only time can ease. When she comes through the door this evening, there will be no mistaking the outcome of the auditions. If her face is joyous, I don't have to worry. But if she comes in with that tight-jawed look she gets when she's hurting, I'll not say anything. I'll remember to respect her pain by not trying to cure it. Instead, I'll hold her—if she lets me.

When I Don't Listen

A fool takes no pleasure in understanding, but only in expressing his opinion.

—Proverbs 18:2

"**B**ut you don't understand!" they wail, and I firmly, evenly tell them I do understand, but the answer is still no. Again, I explain my reasons for the no, and again they argue their point of view and tell me I don't understand.

Often they're right—I don't understand. Oh, I think I do. I can comprehend their wanting something or wanting to do something. I understand it might be embarrassing to bow out of plans they've made with friends. But mostly, I think, they want to win.

The idea of winning is too often mine. I've made a snap decision, and when it's challenged I struggle to defend it with mature reasoning. I tell my children I'm listening to their point of view, and I am—on one level only. Their words and meaning are taken in, but as I listen to their logic I'm using it to counter and defend my turf. I end up feeling bad about saying no when they've given me good reasons for saying yes. I don't feel much better if I relent and allow them what they want because it's due to exhaustion more than good sense.

It would be better to ask first for their reasoning, then to honestly try to understand, and only then to give them a yes or no. A yes might come more easily if I hear them out, and a no would be more fair, not tinged with guilt. There is no issue here that I need to win. My children already recognize my power as a parent; that's why they ask my permission. A parent's yes is as strong as a no.

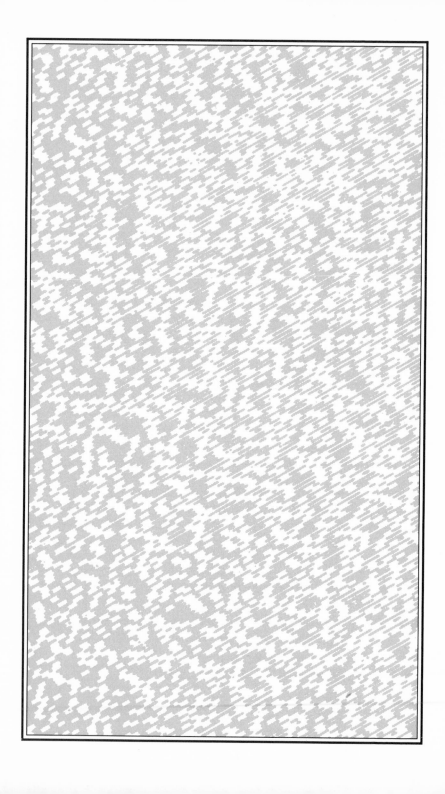

I'd Hate To Be Raising Children Today

Everybody, my friend, everybody lives
for something better to come.
—Maxim Gorky

Almost from the time the first visitor peeked in at our infant daughter and offered congratulations, I've heard the same tag line—"but I sure wouldn't want to be raising kids today." The implication (or sometimes the outright statement) is, life is tough now, there are too many ways a child can go bad, the world is a frightening place in which to bring these innocent babes.

And they're right. I'd have to be living in a house with boarded-up windows to think otherwise. The ways in which the world might hurt my children and the ways in which they can hurt themselves dwarf those mild temptations and dangers I faced as a child. I was in college before I was offered an alcoholic drink; my daughter was in seventh grade. Other drugs, which I knew the names of only from movies, are available in our small town of 1,100 if the right people are asked. My children are media-blitzed by what I believe are distorted sexual messages which promote irresponsibility to self and others. Short of boarding up our windows and safely huddling inside with my daughter and sons, I have little control over how the world threatens them. But they have to live in the world, as do I, and in recognizing that fact I've discovered we have some choice and control in *how* we live in it by deciding *what* we wish to see in it.

For too long I saw only the dangers—misuse of nuclear power, erosion of the family, chemical dependency, and sexual permissiveness. My mistake was in nostalgically looking backward to a supposed better time, a simpler time, and not seeing the wonders of the world today. Listening to and watching my children teaches me that today is a better world than the one in which I lived my childhood.

Contrary to the outcries of adults about the declining values of young people, today's youth are more accepting of others whom we would have labeled as weird. Their modern world has fostered in them a greater sensitivity toward other human beings and developed in them a broader perspective of the world. Even grade school children today are aware of the need to protect the environment and to conserve all plant and animal life on the planet. Today's children are less parochial than we were. Although they have the same loyalties as we had to family, hometown, and nation, they have been gifted with a clearer vision of those institutions as they mesh within a larger image of the world. They see each other more accurately by looking beyond obesity, acne, odd clothes, and family position. Admittedly, they whine and cajole for fad clothes and all the trappings needed for conformity. In that, they're not so different from us, but they're not as judgmental as we were; they're not as afraid of being different. The world today allows that. What many people might dismiss as mouthiness, disrespect, or sassiness is often—not always—evidence of self-respect and a healthy self-image. Today's world encourages children to trust themselves and their feelings—and to speak up.

The confidence and caring within our young people compel my optimism and support my faith that an even better society can await my children's children. The openness, acceptance, and sensitivity of our youth weren't created by the young people themselves; they were fostered by my contemporaries who were willing to parent with greater openness, acceptance, and sensitivity. The social atmosphere that has nurtured these traits has probably contributed to what I see as threats to my children, but a return to the "good old days" is not a healthy solution. As tempting as it is to wrap my children into the same safe cocoon that protected my childhood, I find the price to be too great. If I can't give them that safety without stripping them of the growth I've wanted them to have, I opt to let them live with the dangers. I can't see myself as a human being whose function it is to re-create replicas of myself; I'm a person with a mind and a soul designed to dream and build a better world. My children are not better than I was, but instead they have a better environment in which their best can flourish. So often I tell them that life is constantly getting better for me, deeper, more meaningful. I hope they understand some day that my commitment to this belief was most fully affirmed in my willingness—even eagerness—to raise children in today's world.

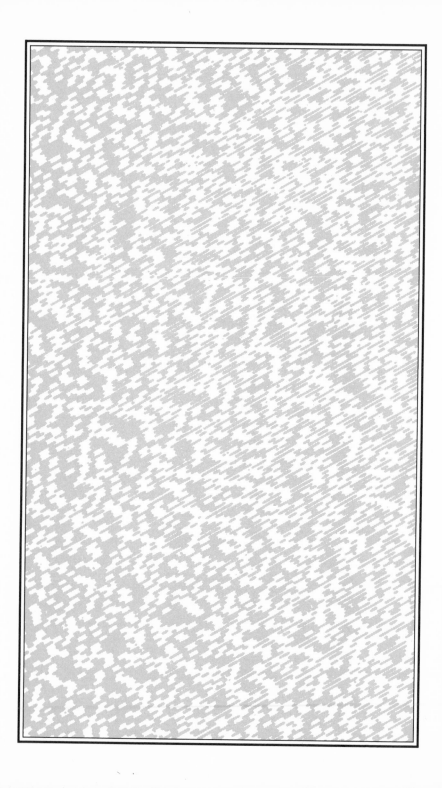

Strawberry Geraniums

*Self-love is the instrument of our
preservation; it resembles the provision
for the perpetuity of mankind; it is
necessary, it is dear to us, it gives us
pleasure, and we must conceal it.*
—Voltaire

My excursion into indoor horticulture was
short-lived, as were the plants I'd en-
thusiastically collected. Most lasted such
a short time I had little chance to even learn their names.
"The green curly-leafed thing looks sick," I'd say, and
within the next day or two I'd be unceremoniously
dumping the green curly-leafed thing into the garbage.
My husband, thinking himself cute, would tell our
friends that I was into dried plants. I was self-conscious,
perhaps even ashamed, of my plants' failure to thrive.
I attempted to conceal their early demise by disposing
of them when no one else was around and by sometimes
secretly replacing them with slightly larger versions. We
were not wealthy people, and this latter practice had
to be abandoned when the pyramiding costs of replacing larger and larger plants forced me to choose between
buying food and buying plants. It was at this point that
I announced my intention to cut back on indoor garden-
ing and to only keep the few I really loved.

Choosing the plants I loved most was simple: I kept
the ones that lived. To this day our house has a few
strategically placed green things, and I'm proud to say
I know their names. Our philodendron—the camel of
the plant world—will survive without water for days and
occasionally for weeks. When deprived, it begins to sulk
and lie down limply in protest. From time to time, it
will play upon my guilt by throwing down a leaf or two,
but it is forgiving. Once again watered, it crisps up in
a day or two just to please me and to impress guests.

129

My grape ivy has many of the same traits as the philodendron, although it probes more deeply into my guilty conscience by feigning death when I depart too far from its watering schedule. For that reason, I'm not as fond of the grape ivy. I don't need that much guilt. But I keep it, partly to reward its tenacious will to survive and partly because I'm in no position to discard a plant that's willing to spring up, green and vital, from its deathbed.

For sentimental reasons, I have a third plant—a strawberry geranium. From the first moment I saw one of these plants, I was enthralled by its gentle parenting nature. A strawberry geranium is usually seen in a hanging pot because it, like a strawberry plant, sends runners out to create new plants. Dozens of small vines cascade over the side, and at the end of each vine is a cluster of leaves—miniatures of the parent plant—each with small roots seeking the earth in which to establish itself. The baby plants hanging helplessly, but nourished perfectly by the parent, appealed to the sense of balance I seemed to need at that time in my life. I bought the first strawberry geranium I saw. I brought it home to brighten a house filled with a mother, a father, two toddlers, and an infant.

I saw my relationship with my children being much the same as that of the geranium and its clusters of small plants. We both nourished and sustained our young— willingly, instinctively, and often at the expense of our well-being. We had created our babies and now were totally responsible for their growth. Somehow the visual balance between the parent plant and its small offspring helped me better understand my new role as parent and made my personal sacrifices easier.

Perhaps *sacrifice* is too strong a word. I didn't give up a multithousand dollar career to become a stay-at-home mother. No education was sacrificed. There were no luring opportunities I refused in deference to parenting.

Change is a better word. Choices changed. Routine changed. My husband and I could no longer make spur-of-the-moment decisions to eat out. We had less alone time together. Less money. Our conversations centered less on romance and more on toilet training and teething pain. I gave up some outside activities and plunged myself into my children's lives. My notion of what parenting meant prompted me to give up many of the elements of what I thought of as "me" in order to become what I thought was a "perfect parent."

Where did the message come from, that I should put my children's wants and needs before my own? The era in which I spent my childhood certainly contributed to it. My family and most others I knew had to make hard financial choices which translated into mothers and fathers forfeiting new clothes, cars, and furniture in order to provide their children with necessities. My mother gave her children classic lessons in self-deprivation by refusing to take the last piece of meat on the platter, by changing her plans to accommodate ours, and by assuring her four offspring that, once you're older, you really do find supreme joy in watching your children open gifts and have no need for any other gift.

There was no one magic moment in which I suddenly realized that parenting wasn't a matter of "them" or "me," that choices which were good for me didn't have to be bad for my children, and that many of the things I could do for myself would also benefit my sons and daughter. I can't even point to a time in which I suddenly began to see my parenting as one part of my life and experience instead of as being all my life. It just happened, and it probably happened gradually as an inner sense of personal survival demanded that I grow.

I haven't become a selfish person, but I have become a fuller, more complete person. I have a more realistic expectation of myself and of my children. We're all human and share those human needs to be loved, cared for, and nourished. In a sense, I not only parent my children, but I also parent myself by acknowledging my needs to grow and to flourish. And my children benefit by being parented by a stronger mother.

Self-love is no longer a source of shame for me, and I don't conceal it. Now, after 45 years of living and seventeen years of parenting, I see it as essential to life as eating and sleeping. It's more of a drive than it is a need. It's what keeps us alive and living fully.

Even my strawberry geranium underlines the truth of this lesson. This plant, that I had at one time seen as the epitome of parental sacrifice and care, is a reminder of the need for self-care, and self-love. Whenever I neglect this tender plant, it begins to die immediately. Unlike the philodendron and the grape ivy that merely droop, the strawberry geranium protects itself by shutting down all extraneous leaves and appendages. The first parts of the plant to wither are the fragile clusters of tiny plants at the end of its runners. When the parent plant is undernourished or underwatered it cannot support the small plants. Like any parent it can't give what it doesn't have. The fragile balance between this plant and smaller plants overrunning its sides reminds me that one way in which I can care for my children is through self-love. It tells me to stay strong. It encourages me to grow. It gives me permission to nurture myself.

Shared Stories

> *Memory is the thing you forget with.*
>
> —*Alexander Chase*

My mother never had a store-bought dress when she was a young girl. She got one pair of shoes a year, and, to make them last, she put cardboard in them in the winter. She had to go barefoot through the summer if she outgrew that one pair. She had to walk something like 48 miles to school. And back. She was given 35 cents a year for school clothes and supplies which forced her to work full-time from the age of nine.

These are the stories I remember hearing whenever I complained about school or my clothes or lack of money. I'd roll my eyes skyward and yawn, and she'd be silenced.

The fact is, we didn't have a lot when I was growing up. I'm sure my clothes were not as nice as the other girls', and I didn't have much spending money for candy or pop. I'm not bitter about it; it's just how it was.

My children, on the other hand, are blessed with up-to-date clothes, allowances, and their own rooms. When they complain, I get angry at their lack of appreciation. One time, in particular, I received a torrent of complaints from them. One son claimed his winter jacket was too small (although he'd worn it the day before), the other had to have ten dollars for skiing, and my daughter had nothing to wear—despite a closet I envy. Their allowances were inadequate, they said; *everyone* gets a bigger allowance. And—they wanted me to drive them to school rather than catch the bus a block away! That was the clincher.

133

I leveled my eyes and my voice to them: "When . . . I . . . was . . . young," I began (they started to squirm), "I walked or rode my bike the mile and a half to school. And back. I went to a country school for five years in which eight grades were all in one room." (I had their attention.) "We carried water from an outside well. On cold winter days, the classroom smelled of scorched wool as our mittens dried atop the wood-burning stove. Our lunches against the wall would be tinged with frost by noontime." (They seemed interested.)

I continued. "We used pencils after the erasers were gone. And we wrote on both sides of the paper." (Skepticism flashed across their faces.) "We didn't wear tennis shoes. Or makeup. Our jeans had no labels on the backsides, and the girls' jeans zipped up the side. Our shirts had no writing or pictures on them."

It was then that I caught them rolling their eyes full circle and looking sidelong at each other, and I stopped. I'd gone too far.

Eventually, I'll tell them these stories again. And there are others that I know they'll enjoy. It's somehow comforting to know that they'll remember my childhood experiences as vividly as I recall their grandmother's.

Just So I'm Healthy

Our entire life, with our fine moral code and our precious freedom, consists ultimately of accepting ourselves as we are.

—*Jean Anouilh*

No statistics exist to tell us what are the most-used phrases in our language. "Have a nice day" certainly must be a contender (especially if "Have a good weekend"—Friday's parting words—is included in that total). "How are you?" and "Let's get together soon" must be up there too. My own personal favorite is "Just so it's healthy." I estimate that this is said almost twenty million times each year. The only statistics available to support the popularity of this phrase are the fact that the number of pregnancies in the past year is just shy of four million and that I'm estimating every parent must say "I don't care which sex it is, just so it's healthy" at least twice per pregnancy. And that, I think, is a very conservative estimate.

I said it and, like most new mothers, I quickly checked and counted each of my babies' fingers and toes the first time I held her or him. At that moment, normalcy and averageness were all I asked for. They didn't have to be geniuses or beautiful, just healthy and normal.

It's probably unfortunate for me that those infants continued to be normal, because now they all are in various stages of what I've been told is normal—embarrassment about their parents, particularly their mother. The first stage for all of them was displeasure about my age. What they thought I could do about it, I'm not sure, but they all became ashamed of my age when they were about ten or twelve. My older son at the precocious age of nine let me know how much he envied his friend whose mother was 29. His friend couldn't believe it, my son said, that I was not only older, but ten years older than she. My son was truly humiliated. As swept up as he was in his nine-year-old selfishness, he couldn't accept my argument that even if I could have had him at age nineteen or twenty, it would have been very inconvenient since I didn't marry until I was 26. He sniffed at this logic and carried his grudge for quite some time.

My height was another source of dismay for my children. As my daughter explains it, she didn't realize that she was not terribly short at five-foot-four until she really started looking at other mothers. "I'm taller than a lot of them," she reported, "so I'm not short; you're just too tall." She was especially embarrassed if I insisted on wearing my higher heels when my husband and I went out for dinner because, she claimed, this made me taller than he was. She was currently reading piles of romance books, which gave her a worldly awareness that "his powerful arm" could not "sweep around her and lift her to his chiseled face" if "she" could look down and see the part in "his" hair. My daughter's only consolations were two: she could avoid being seen with her father and me, and she could probably be "lifted" throughout her life since she acquired some diminutive genes from her father's side of the family.

All the children, at some time or another, have tried to avoid being seen with us. I've looked closely at other people at the gatherings we've attended, and it's impossible to see any distinguishable difference between them and us. We wear similar clothes, have similar mannerisms, and look like peas in a pod to me. Yet all our children shunned us in public for a time.

They grow out of that phase, and I trust they'll grow out of all the other embarrassments too. Eventually, they'll no longer be threatened if I talk to a teacher about them. Or if I speak out in public. Or if I make one of my humorous comments to a stranger. (I believe this is one of my communication strengths; they think it's "disgusting.") Maybe they'll be adults before they can accept me as I've accepted them. In fact, I now realize it will go full circle. The day will come when my children, grown and with children of their own, will be content that I am average or normal. By that time they will have come to the understanding that the love shared between parents and children is not dependent on talent, looks, or wealth. It is just there. In much the same way that I only asked that my children be healthy, my children some day will pray the same thing for me.

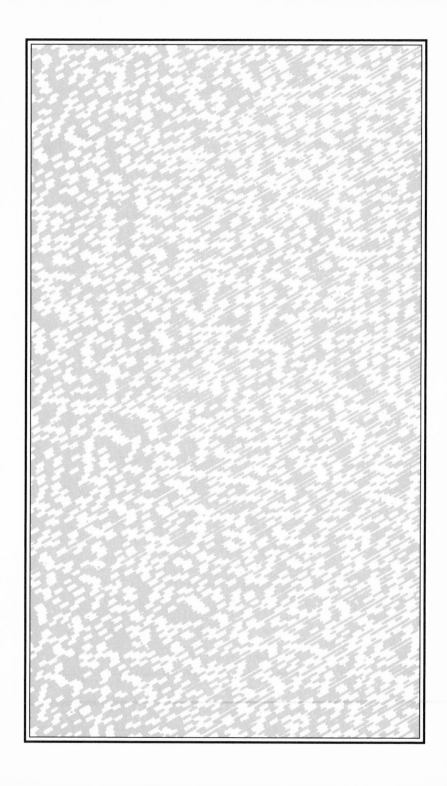

Masterpieces

Now I really make the little idea from clay, and I hold it in my hand. I can turn it, look at it from underneath, see it from one view, hold it against the sky, imagine it any size I like, and really be in control almost like God creating something.

—Henry Moore

From the moment each baby was first cradled in my arms, I was overwhelmed with the responsibility resting there. The forming, the teaching, the creating of this individual were, I believed, my duty as a parent.

I saw my babies as incomplete personalities waiting to be molded. They were clean, untouched canvases on which I was asked to create masterpieces. Their outcome depended totally on my brush strokes: a liberal, daring application of oil with palette knife would create one personality, while a conservative use of color and form would create another. It all depended on me, and I was limited only by time and natural parenting talent.

It was many years later before I recognized my mistake. Foolishly I had worked to perfect my creativity and had felt guilty for my failures to form, on canvas, what I saw so clearly in my mind. Then, suddenly it seemed, I saw that what I had been given were not blank canvases; my masterpieces—my children—were more like computer cards—like those cards which can be held up to the light to show all the prepunched information encoded there. A hole here might mean a stubborn nature; the hole over there might be humor.

With this new awareness, so much of my parenting experience made sense. These children had been placed in my care with imprinted personalities. This meant that one son's temper tantrums that began at eight months weren't necessarily a brush or palette error, nor was the gentle, sharing nature of that same boy an expression of my creativity. All or most of their personalities were preformed. It was always there to see had I only looked. God has already created each child as a unique expression of His love. My responsibility is to nurture, not re-make, these individual personalities. I must not staple, fold or mutilate. I'm not the artist; I'm only the caretaker.

Wishful Thinking

Could everything be done twice
everything would be done better.
—German Proverb

*I*f only I could start over. At one point in my life, I was consumed with such wishful thinking, especially when I considered my years of parenting. If only. If only I could have them as babies again. I'd write detailed and wondrous descriptions in their baby books. I'd hold them closer and longer. I'd read to them more. I'd play with them more. If only they were toddlers again...I'd take them for walks. I'd have spontaneous winter picnics on the living room floor. I'd take more pictures of them. I'd put the ones I took into albums. If only I could start over again, I'd give them piano lessons and let them stay up later with us at night. I'd set aside a night each week for family activities. I'd give more encouragement to those special gifts within each of them.

Age has some advantages, and one of them is I'm better able to see the futility of wishful thinking. It helped me little, and my children not at all, to anguish over past mistakes or oversights. And dragging the burden of an imperfect past prevented me from making a better present. I still lapse from time to time into these self-defeating thoughts, wishing I could repeat portions of my life and do them better the second time around. Admittedly, given another go-round, I would be a stronger parent, just as I would be a more caring daughter, a harder-working student, and a less-selfish newlywed.

Those chances never come, but new opportunities are given me. Each day is a gift that allows me to look back and measure my growth. Growth—greater capacity for love, greater acceptance of others and self, higher self-image, less fear, and more kindness—should not be a source of pain or embarrassment when looking back at an earlier stage of life. Growth should be, must be, a source of joy and thanksgiving. The person I am at this moment is not the same person I see in my past. We share the same name, but only part of the same history. The person of the past, her choices, her pains, are like a rigid painting staring with lifeless eyes from a museum wall. I can't change her; I won't judge her. But I—the life-filled creature of here and now—have choices to make and the opportunity to grow. Husband, children, mother, brothers, sister, home, and other relatives and friends are near. Today is another chance. I intend to live it well.

Less-Than-Perfect

Life, we learn too late, is in the tissue
of each day and hour.
—Stephen Leacock

Many well-meaning older friends and family members told me long ago, "Enjoy your children now; they'll be grown up before you know it." If I listened, I didn't understand—until now. Here I am with my children nearly grown, and I'm filled with remorse. So many years had always seemed to stretch ahead, years to fill with wondrous memories—when I had more time. Now, suddenly it seems, they no longer look to me for answers or comfort or a partner in a board game. Sometimes I wish I could start over.

But how would it be different? Would I put off other responsibilities to fully devote myself to them? Quit a job? Take less time for friends? Give less time to my marriage? Parenting doesn't occur in a vacuum with no other demands than providing perfect love for children. Quite often my choices were taken from less-than-perfect options. And even those which weren't best choices or caring choices were made by a parent who was, and is, less than perfect. And for that, I forgive myself.

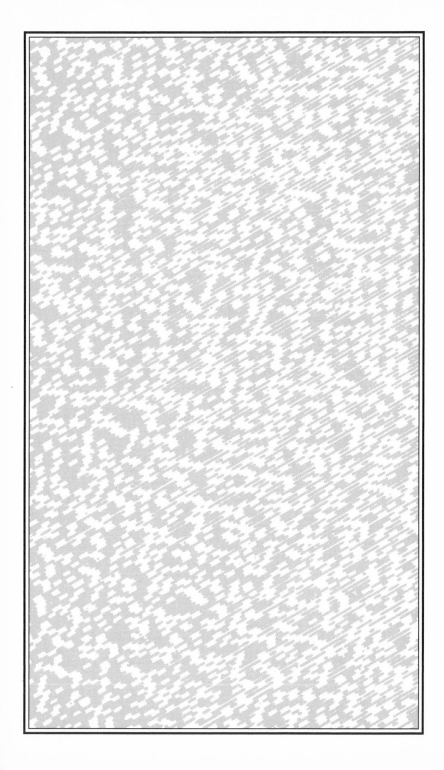

Other titles that will interest you...

Today's Gift
Bring your whole family together for a moment's meditation with *Today's Gift*, a collection of daily meditations written especially for families. Here is a book that nurtures family esteem and strengthens family bonds as it imparts inspiration that has meaning for everyone, no matter how young or old. And topics such as harmony, sharing, individuality, trust, privacy and toleration, will stimulate family discussion. 400 pp. Order No. 1031

Codependent No More
by Melody Beattie
This is the definitive book about codependency, written by a recovering codependent and former family counselor for all of those like her who have suffered the torment of loving too much. Melody Beattie explains what codependency is, what it isn't, who's got it, and how to move beyond it. 208 pp. Order No. 5014

Keeping Promises
The Challenge of a Sober Parent
by Kay Marie Porterfield
As recovering parents, it is important to realize how our chemical use may have affected our relationships with our children. This upbeat book takes a one-day-at-a-time approach to the parenting challenges faced by recovering people. It offers practical suggestions to help us renew family relationships and begin keeping promises to our children for a new, nurturing family life together. 172 pp. Order No. 1032

For price and order information please call one of our Customer Service Representatives

HAZELDEN EDUCATIONAL MATERIALS
(800) 328-9000   **(800) 257-0070**   **(612) 257-4010**
(Toll Free. U.S. Only)   (Toll Free. MN Only)   (AK and Outside U.S.)
Pleasant Valley Road • Box 176 • Center City, MN 55012-0176